The Zombie Coloring Book

By Matthew E. Breer

An adult coloring book, inspired by witty zombie phrases and all things zombie!
Over 40 illustrations for hours of stress relieving fun!
This book makes a perfect gift for everyone!

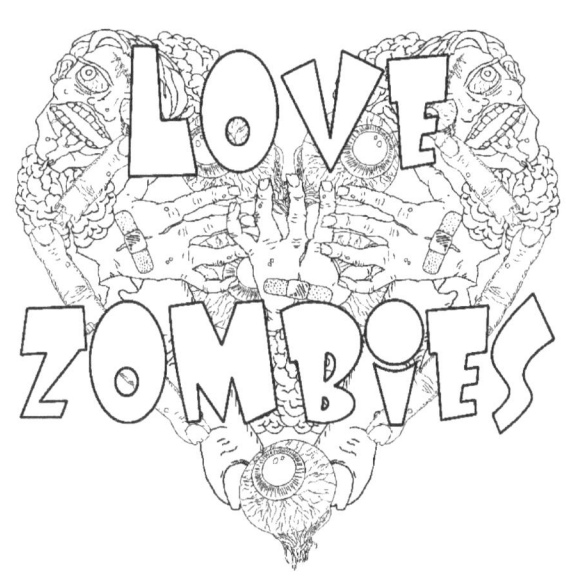

Be sure to check us out on Facebook and our website for other great things!

http://breerspublishing.weebly.com/

https://www.facebook.com/breerspublishing/

Images in this book are created from public domain creative commons, royalty-free vintage art, and original art work.
Copyright 2017 Breer's Art & Things Vintage publishing. All rights reserVED.

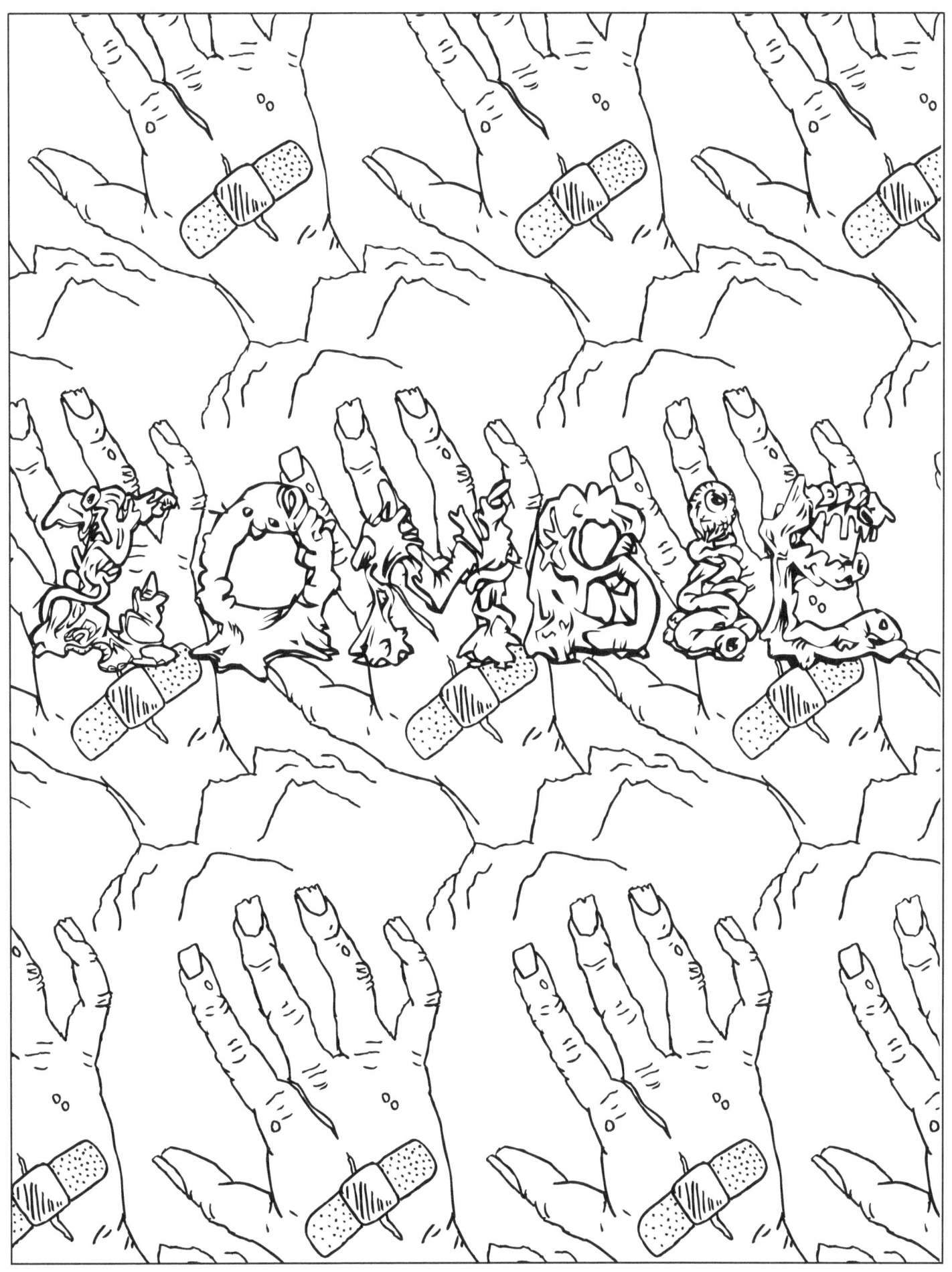

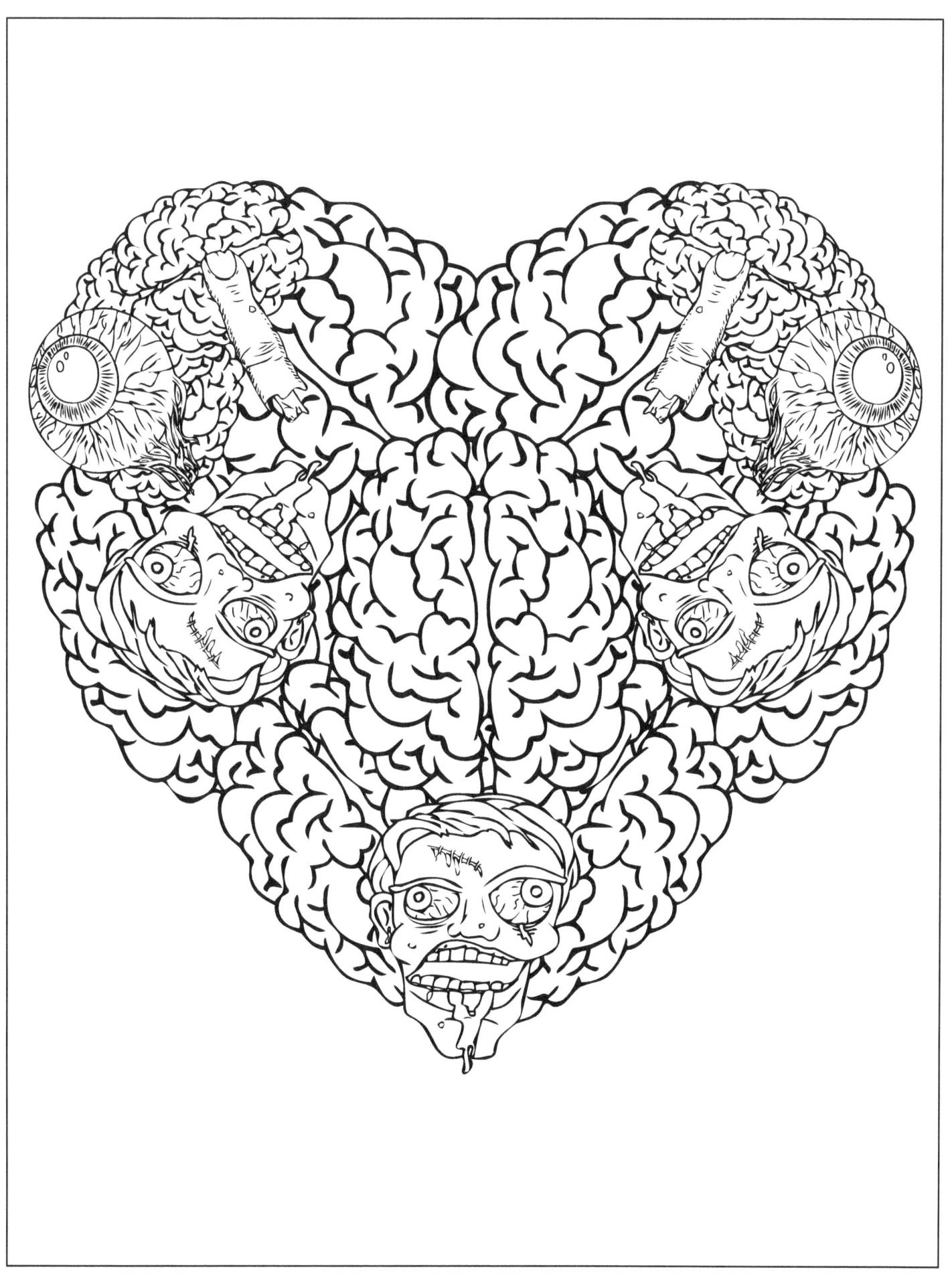

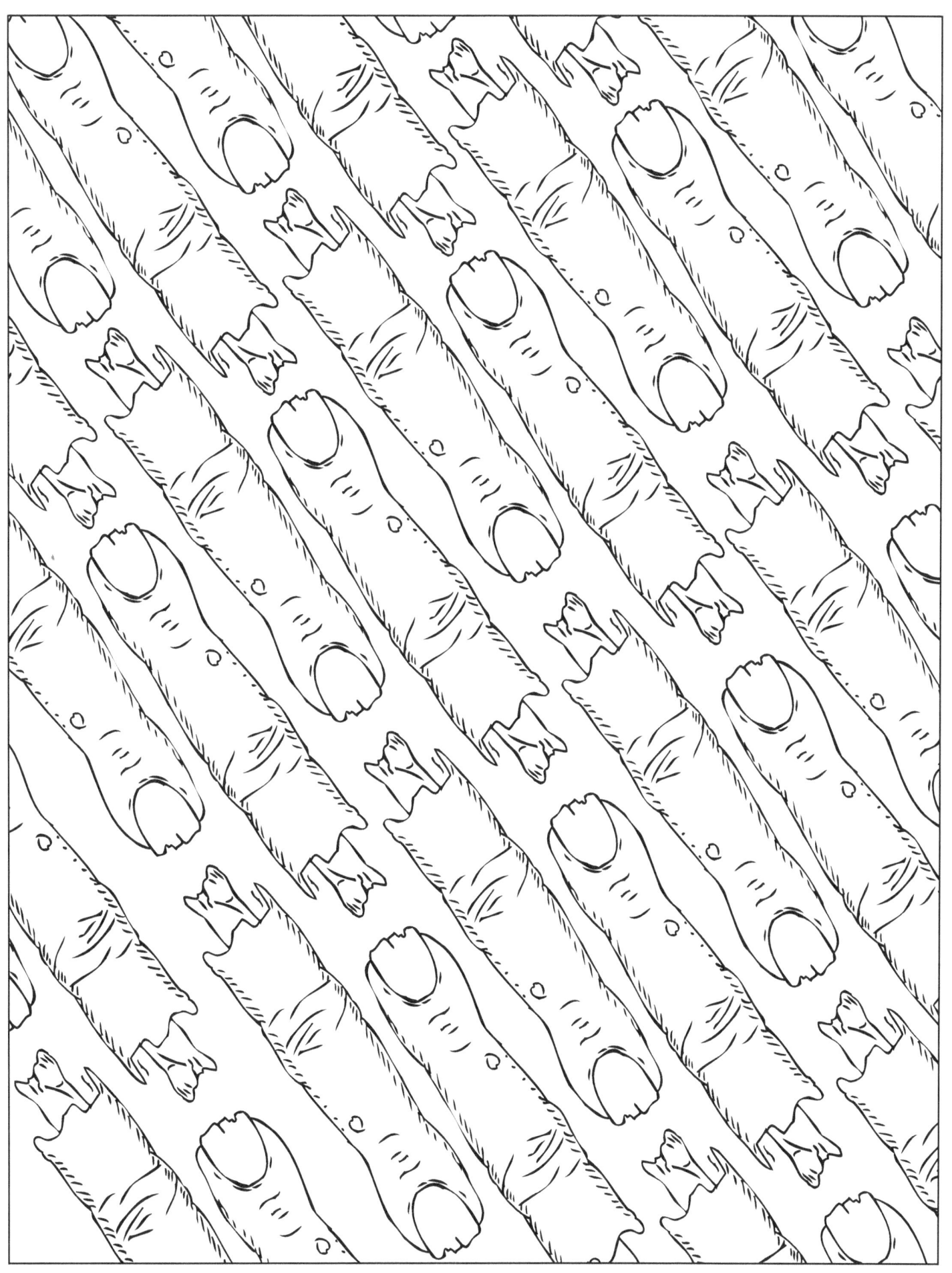

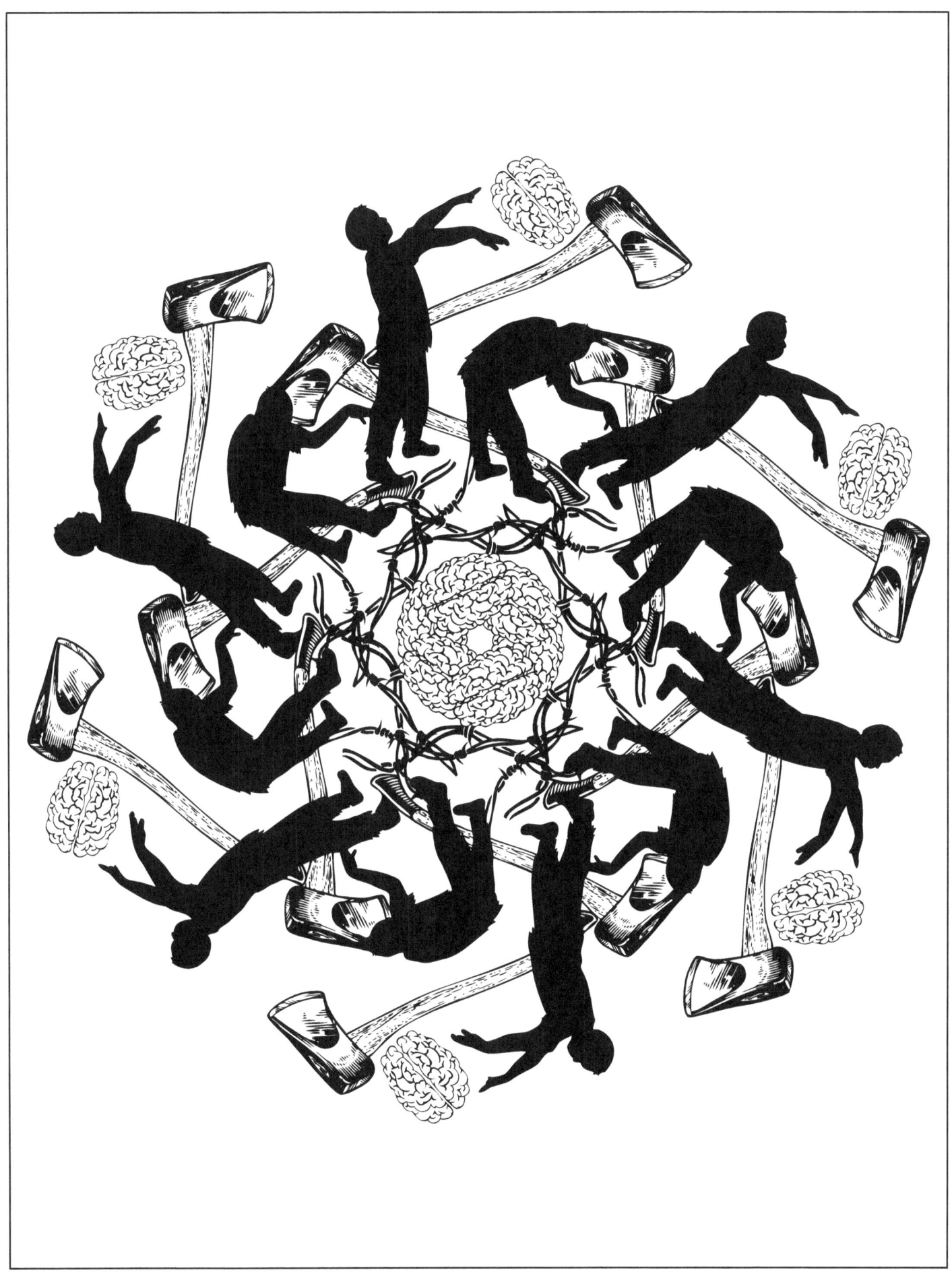

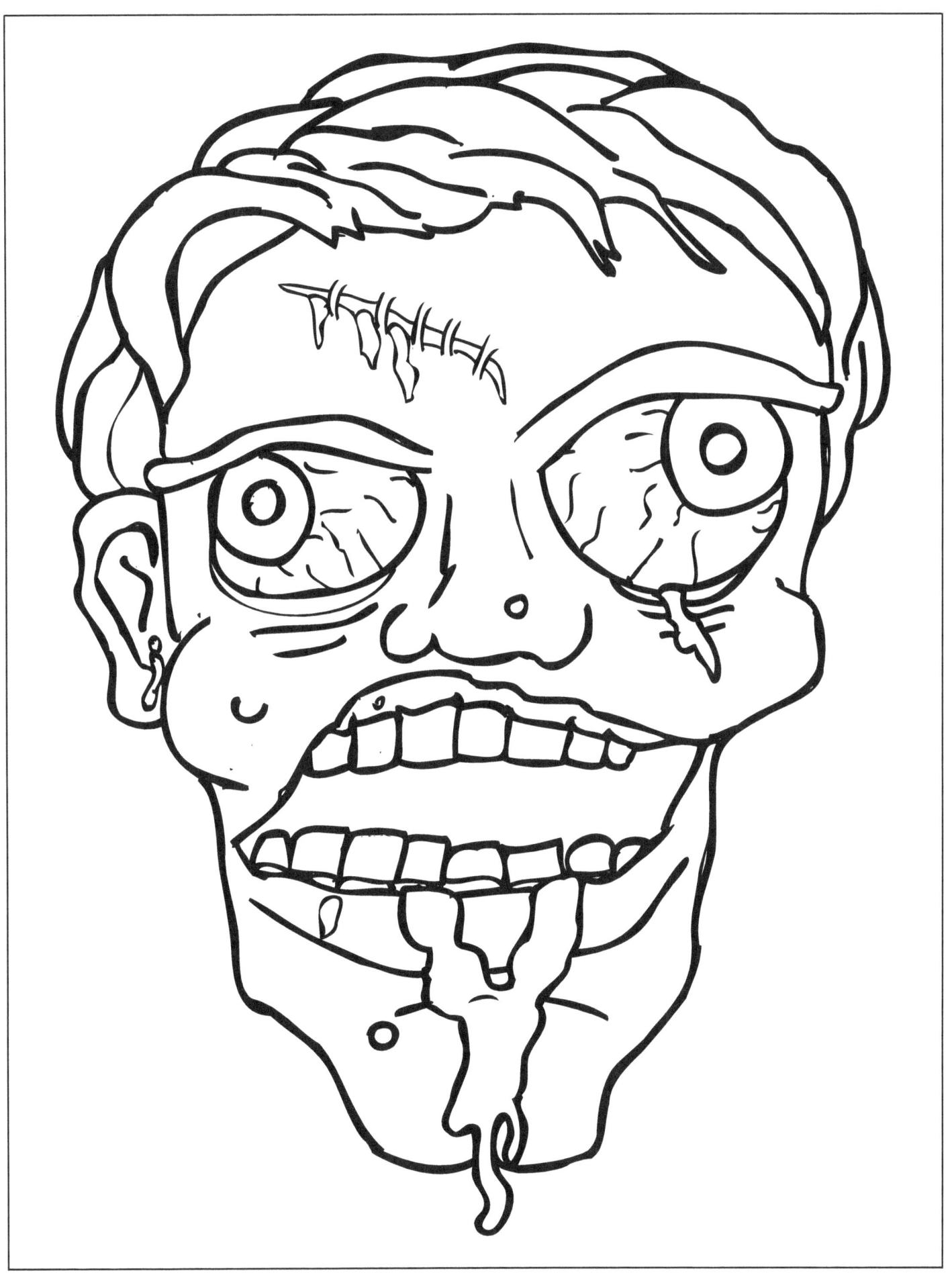

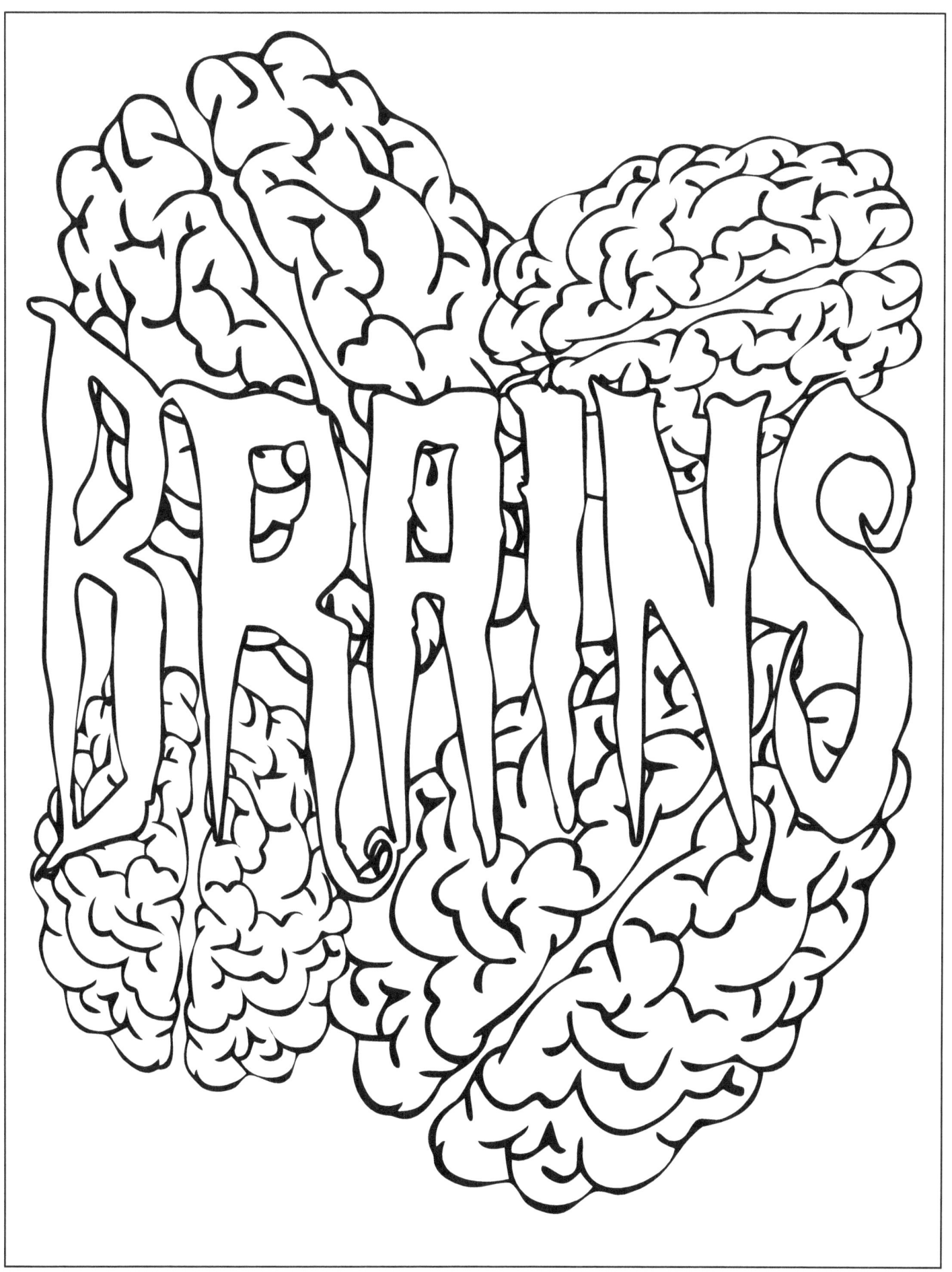

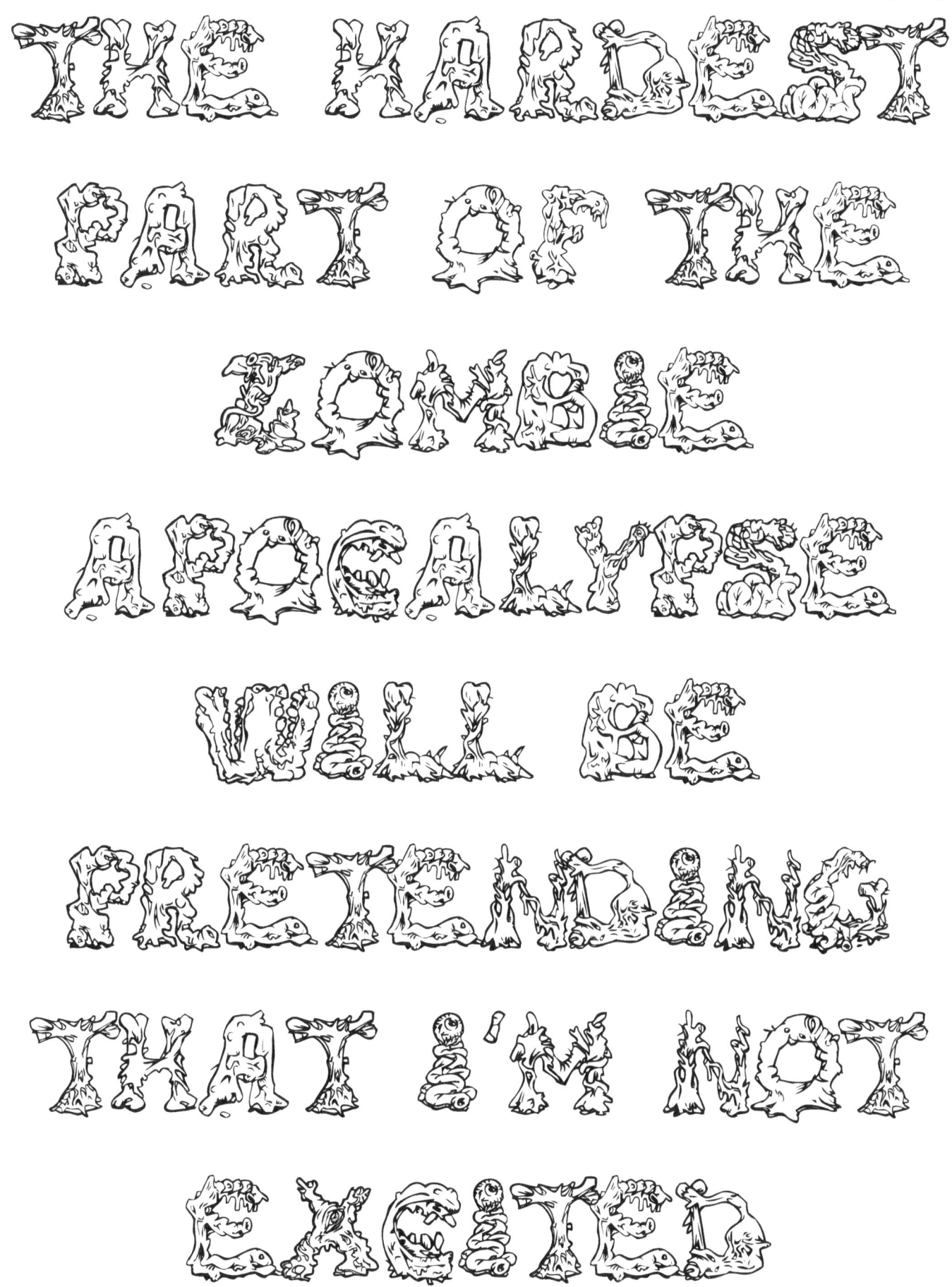

THE HARDEST PART OF THE ZOMBIE APOCALYPSE WILL BE PRETENDING THAT I'M NOT EXCITED

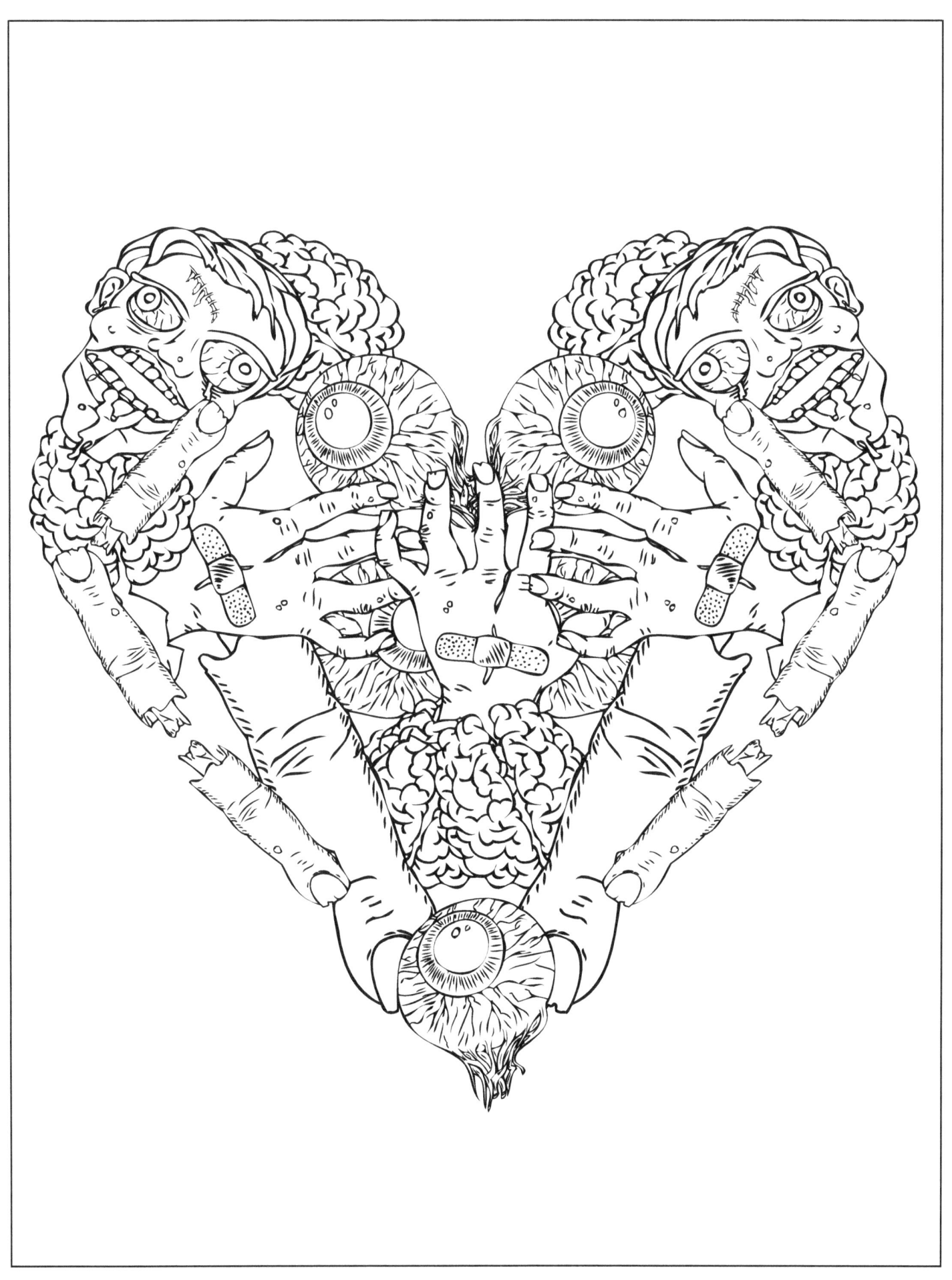

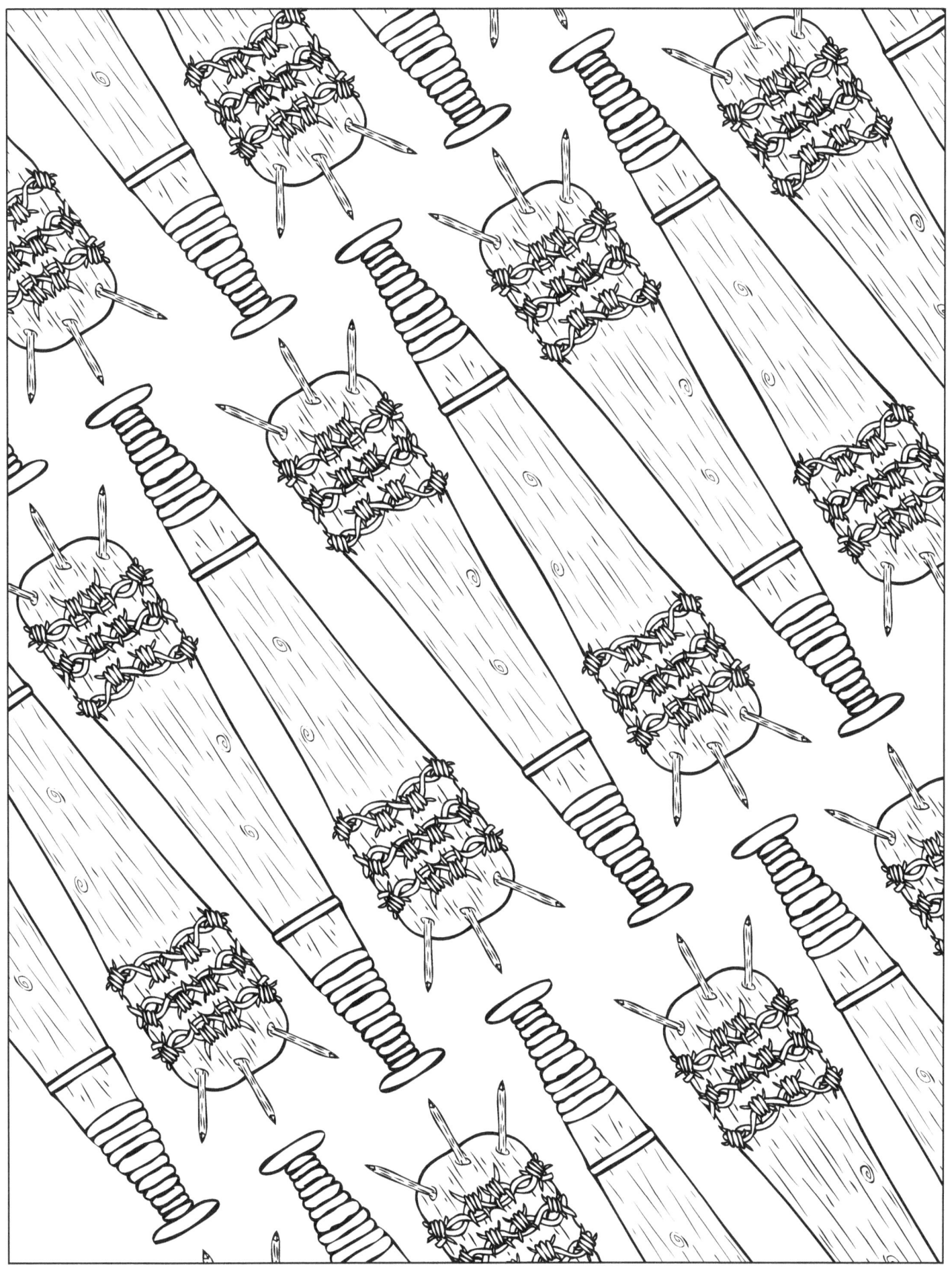

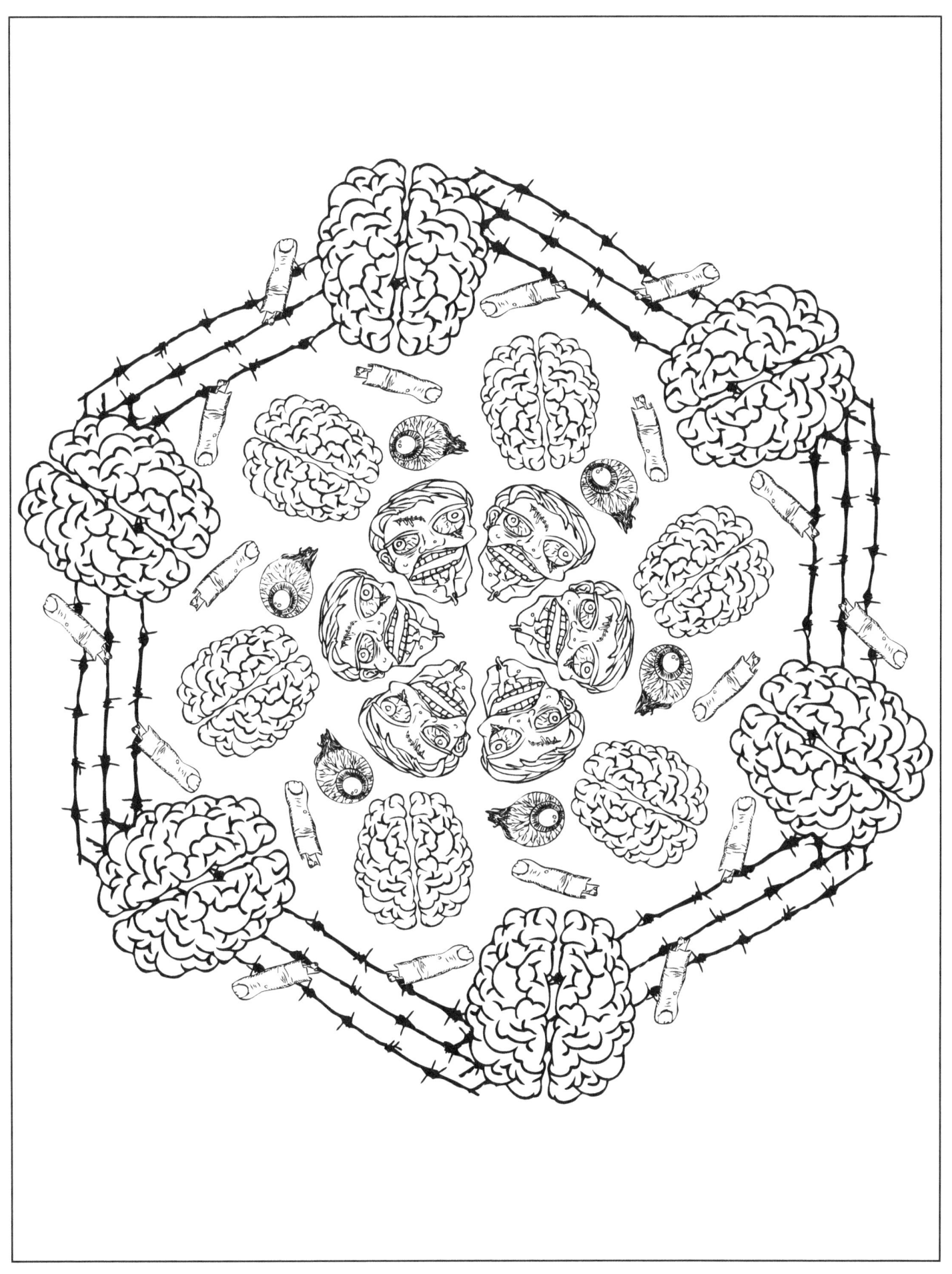

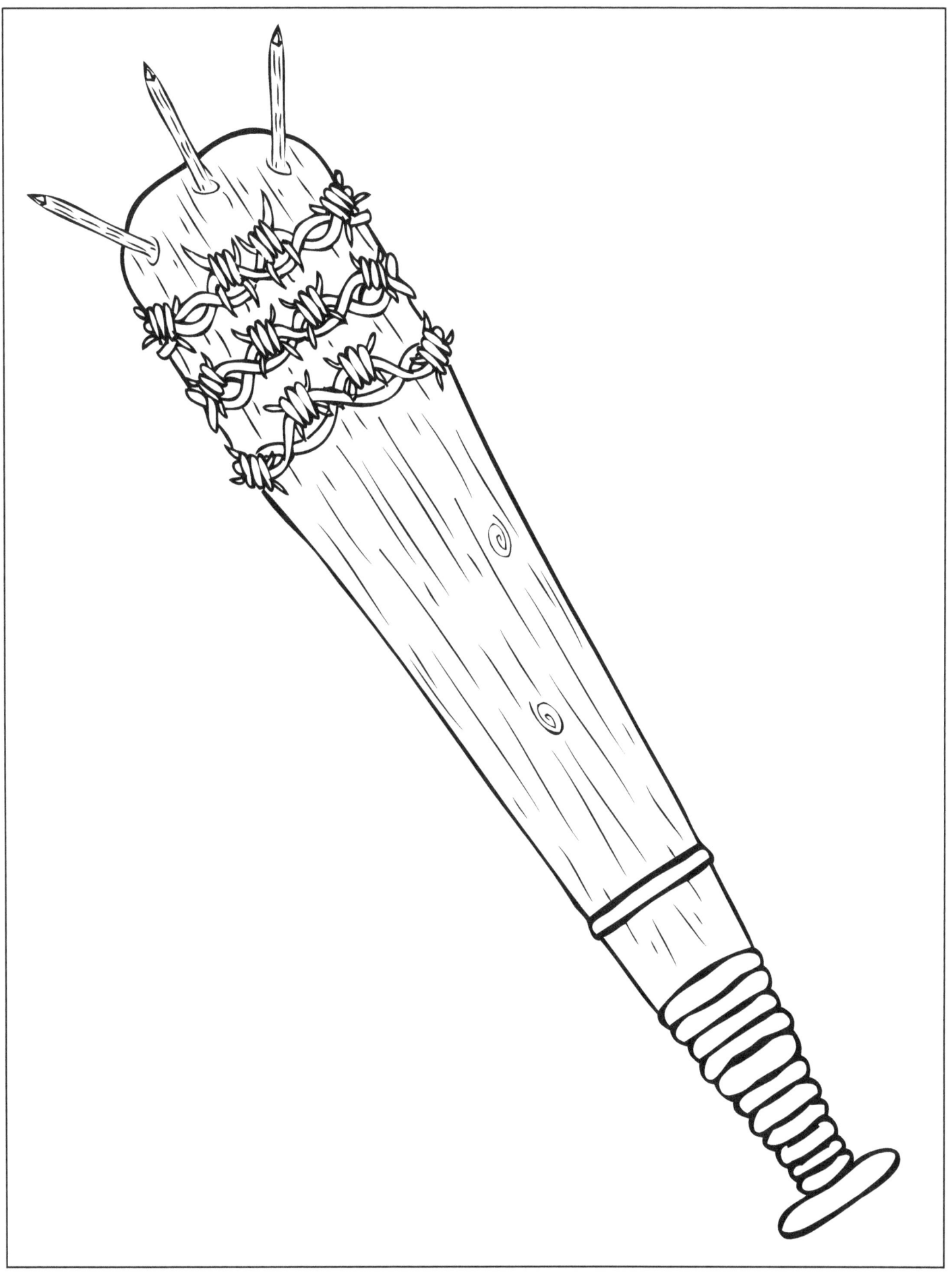

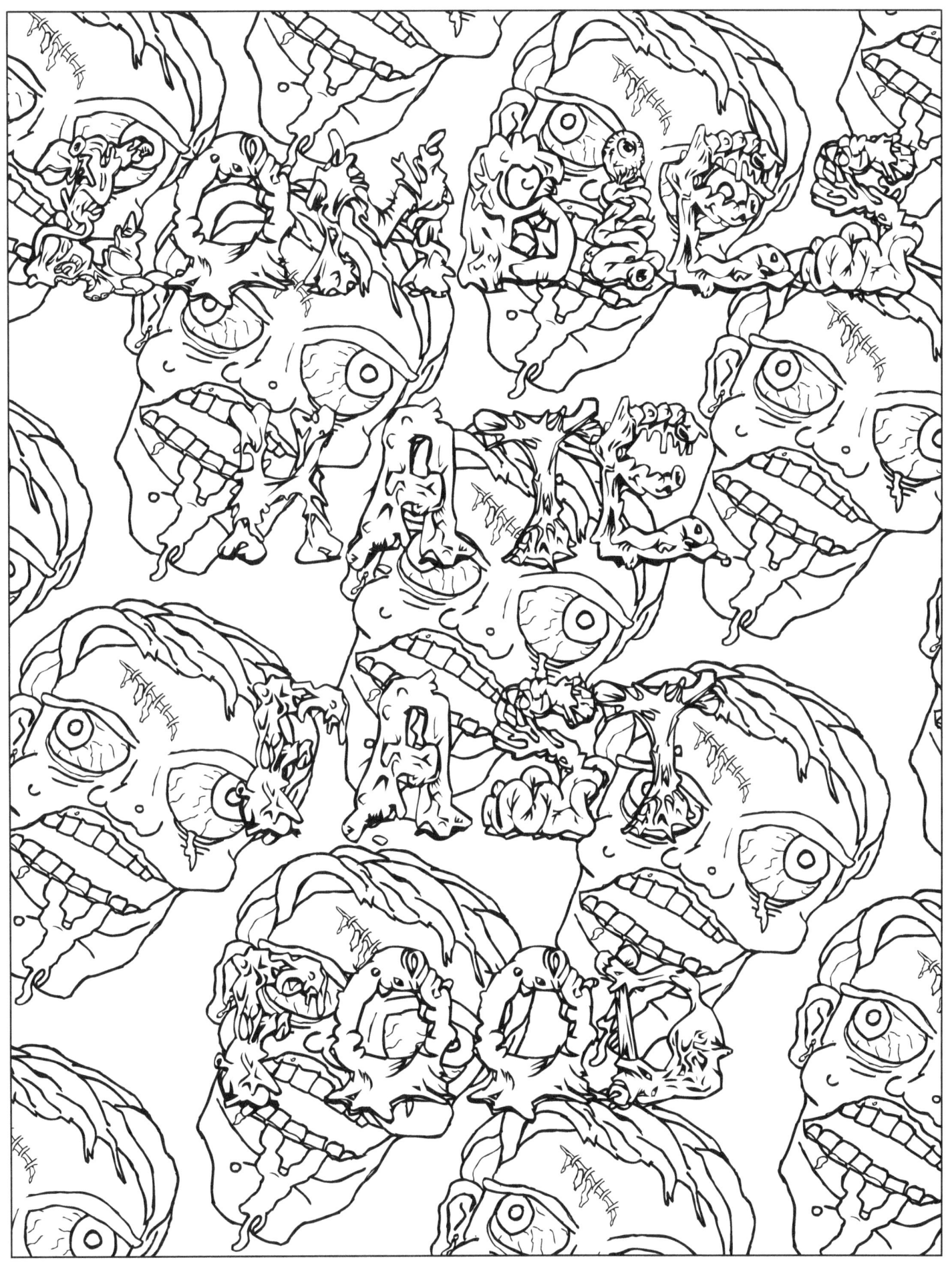

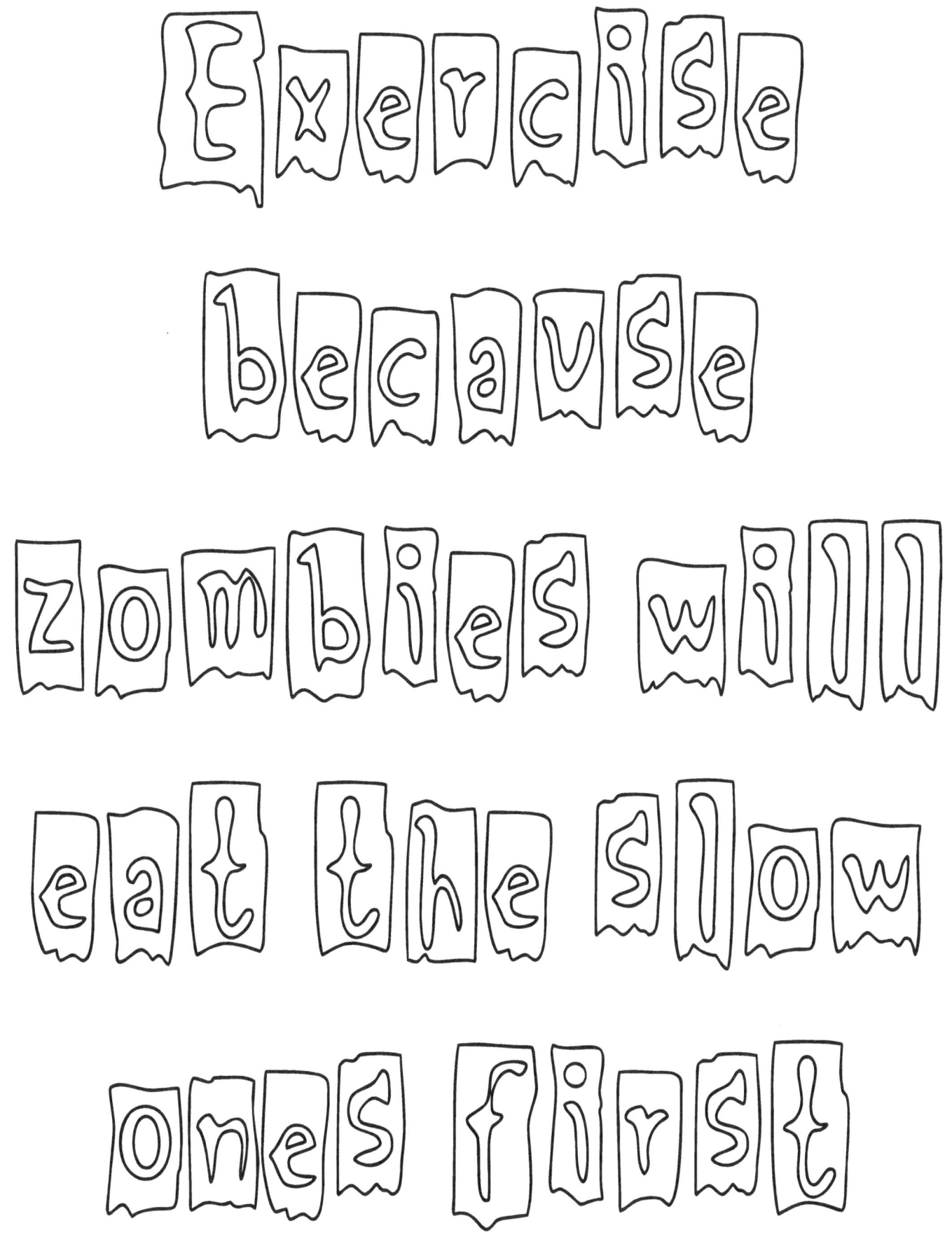

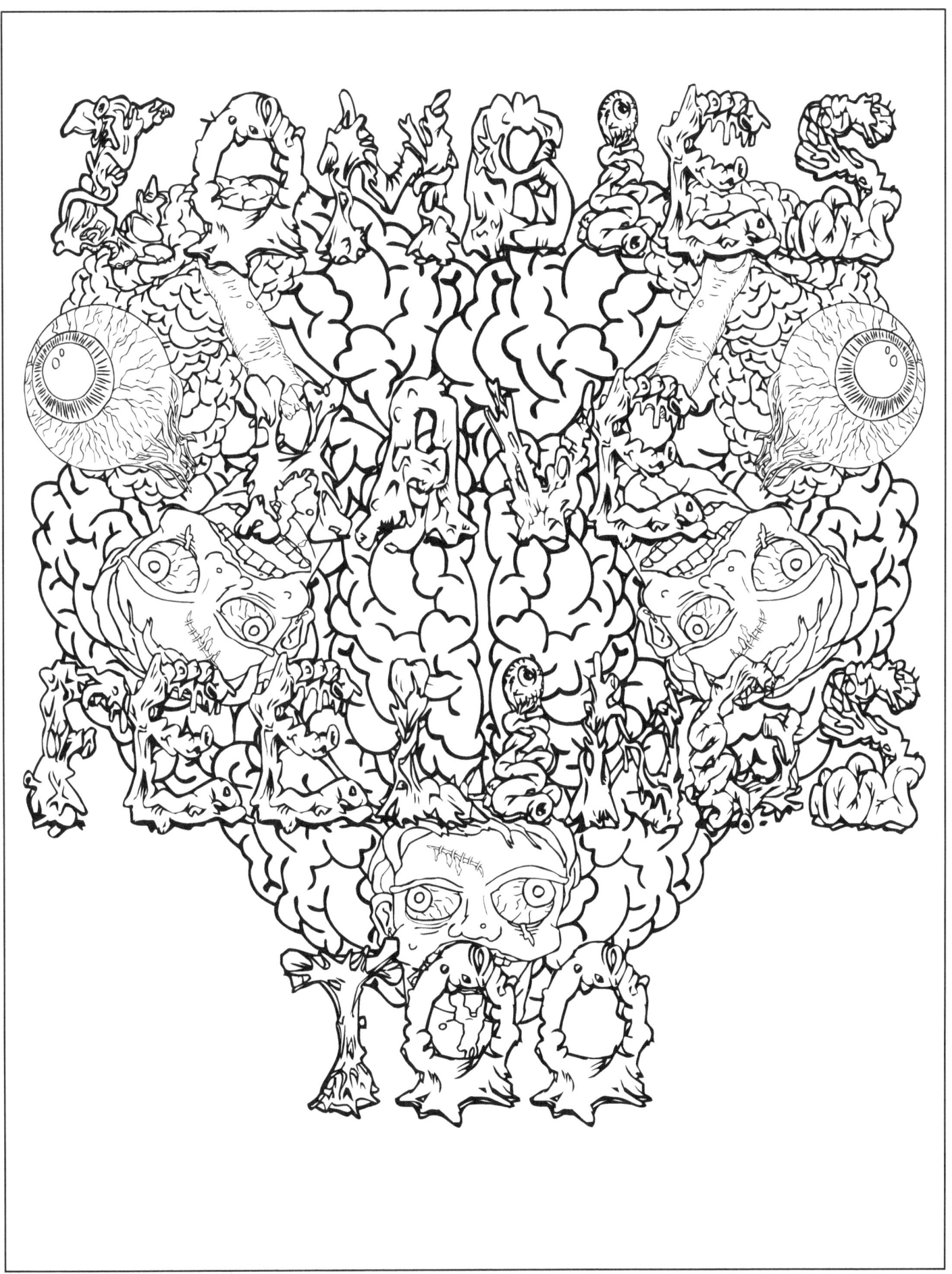

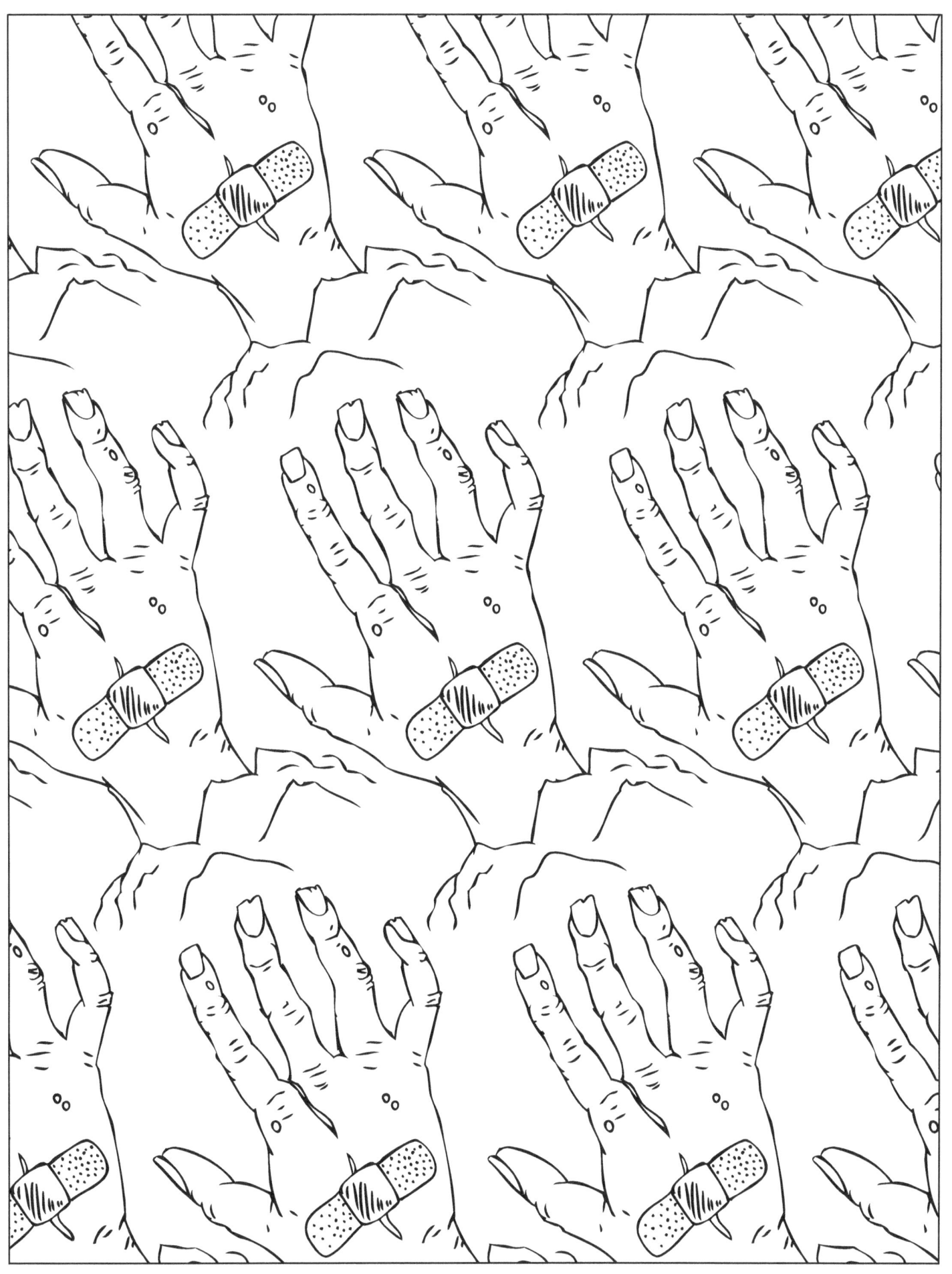

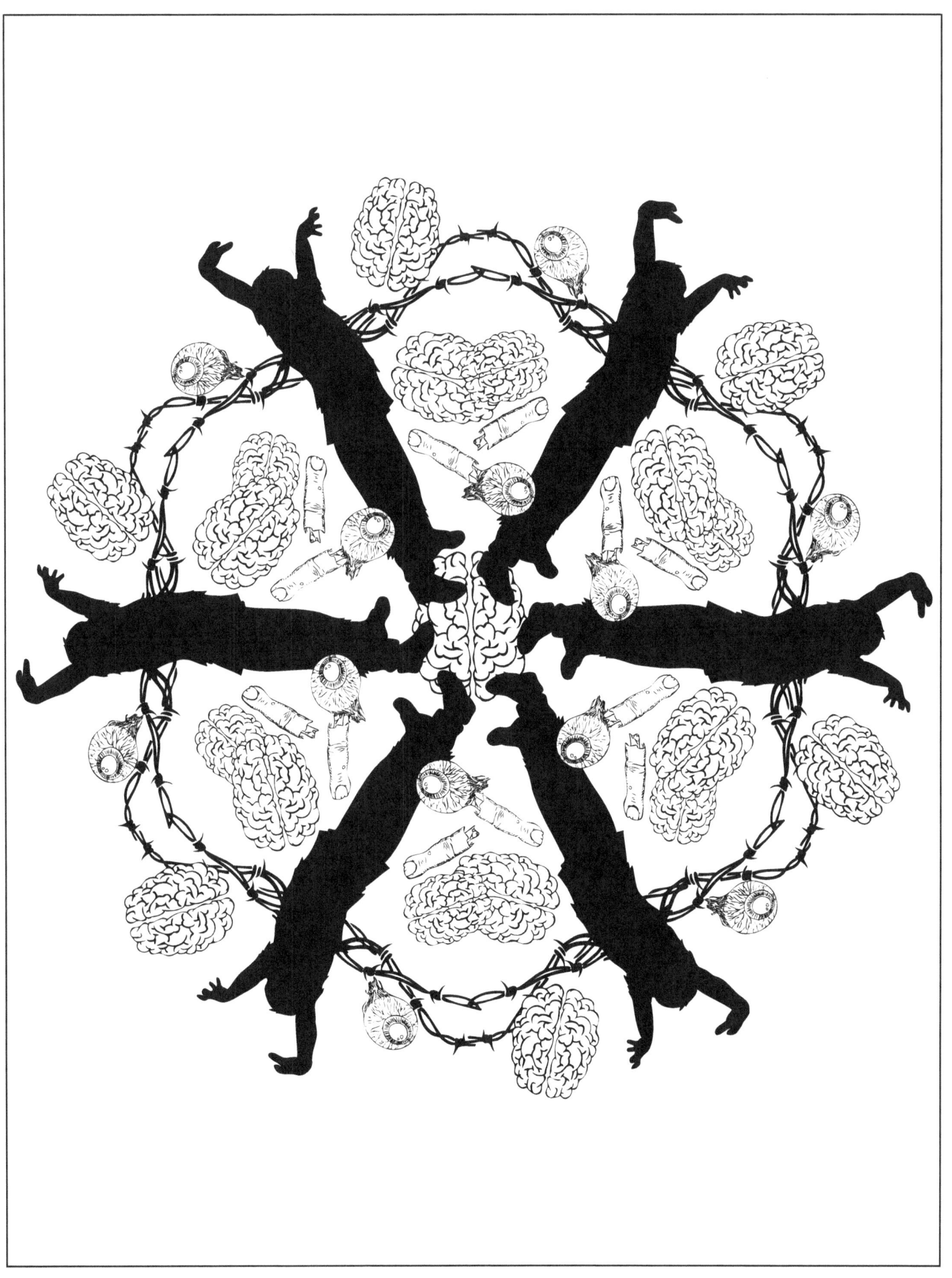

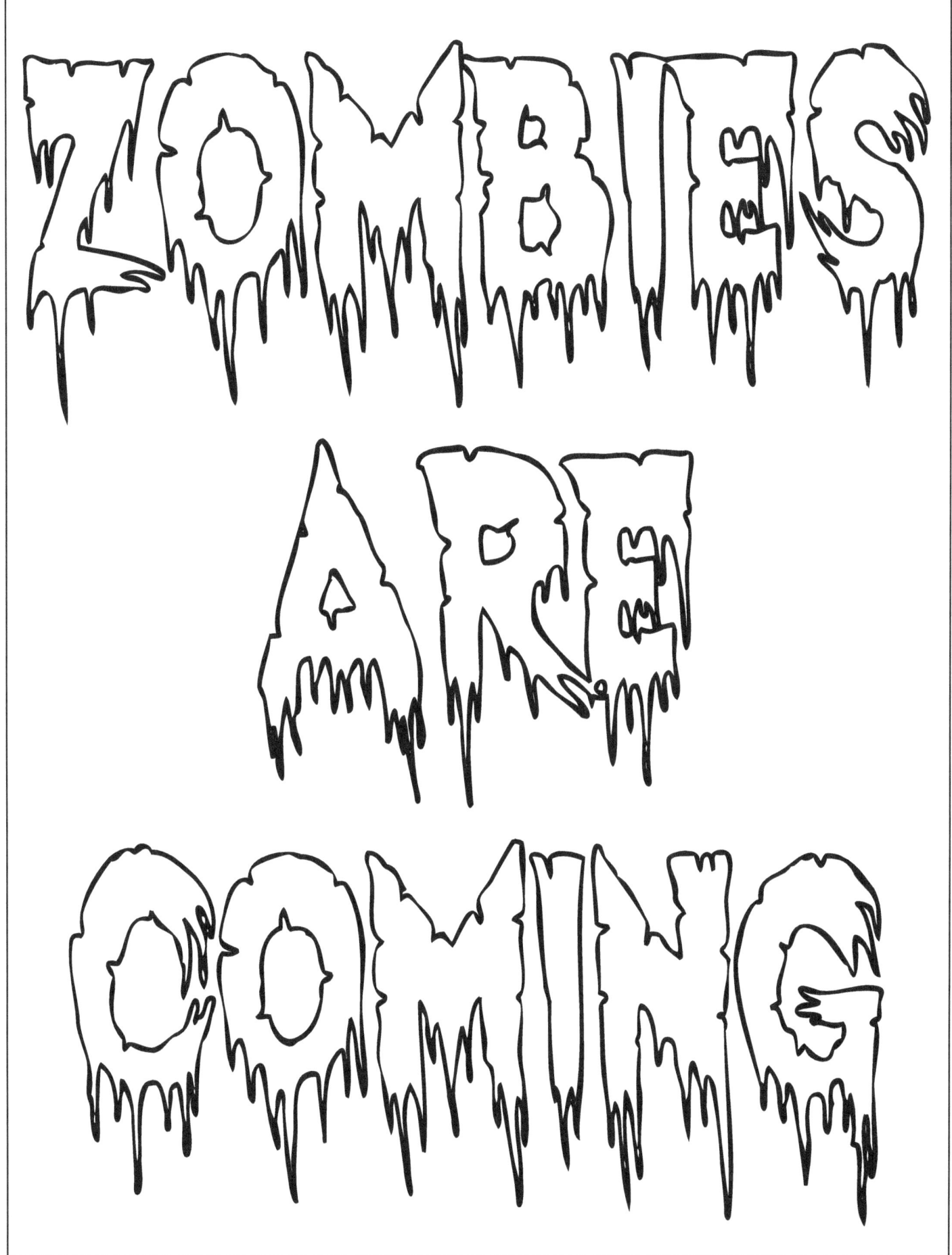

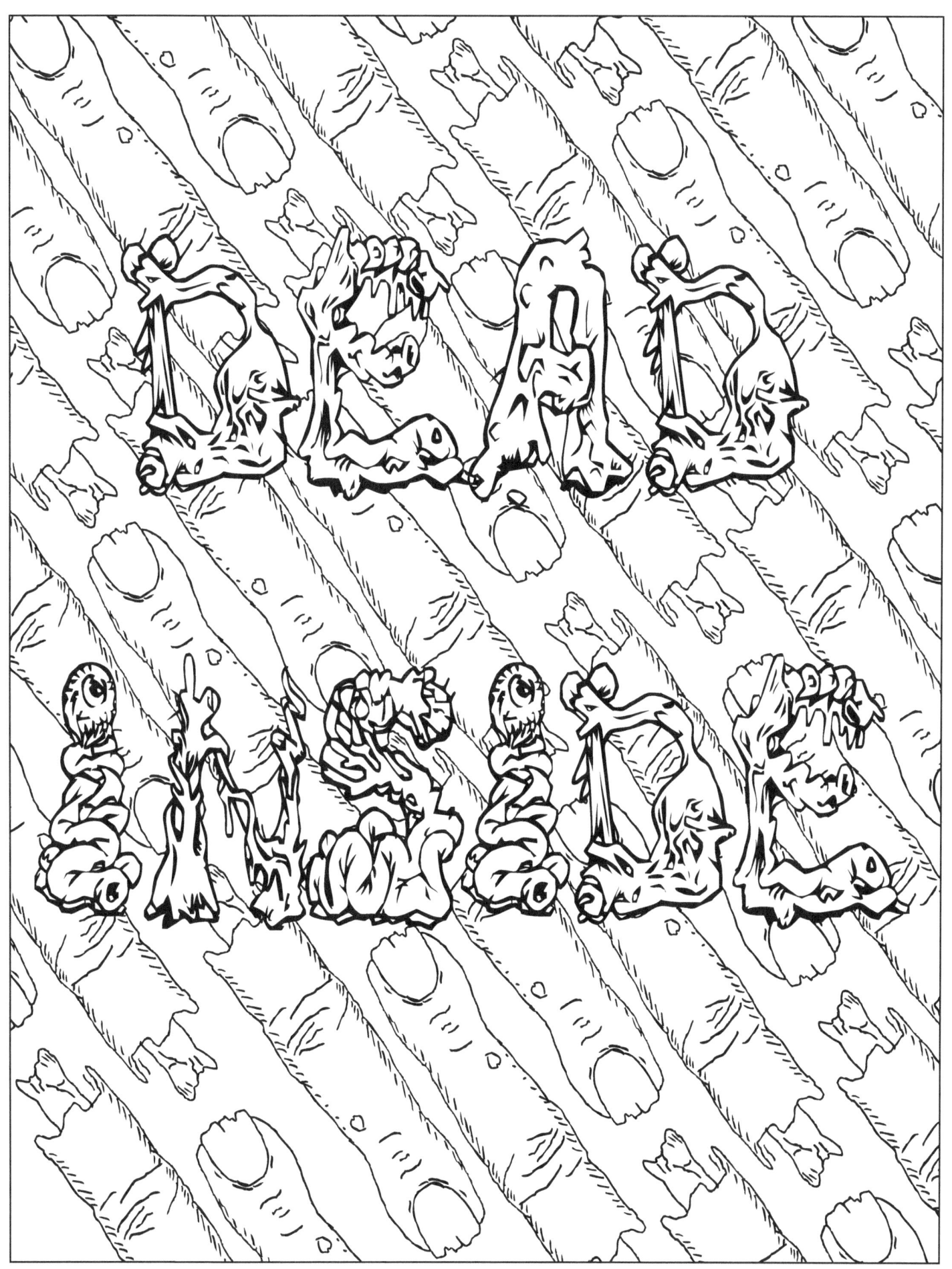

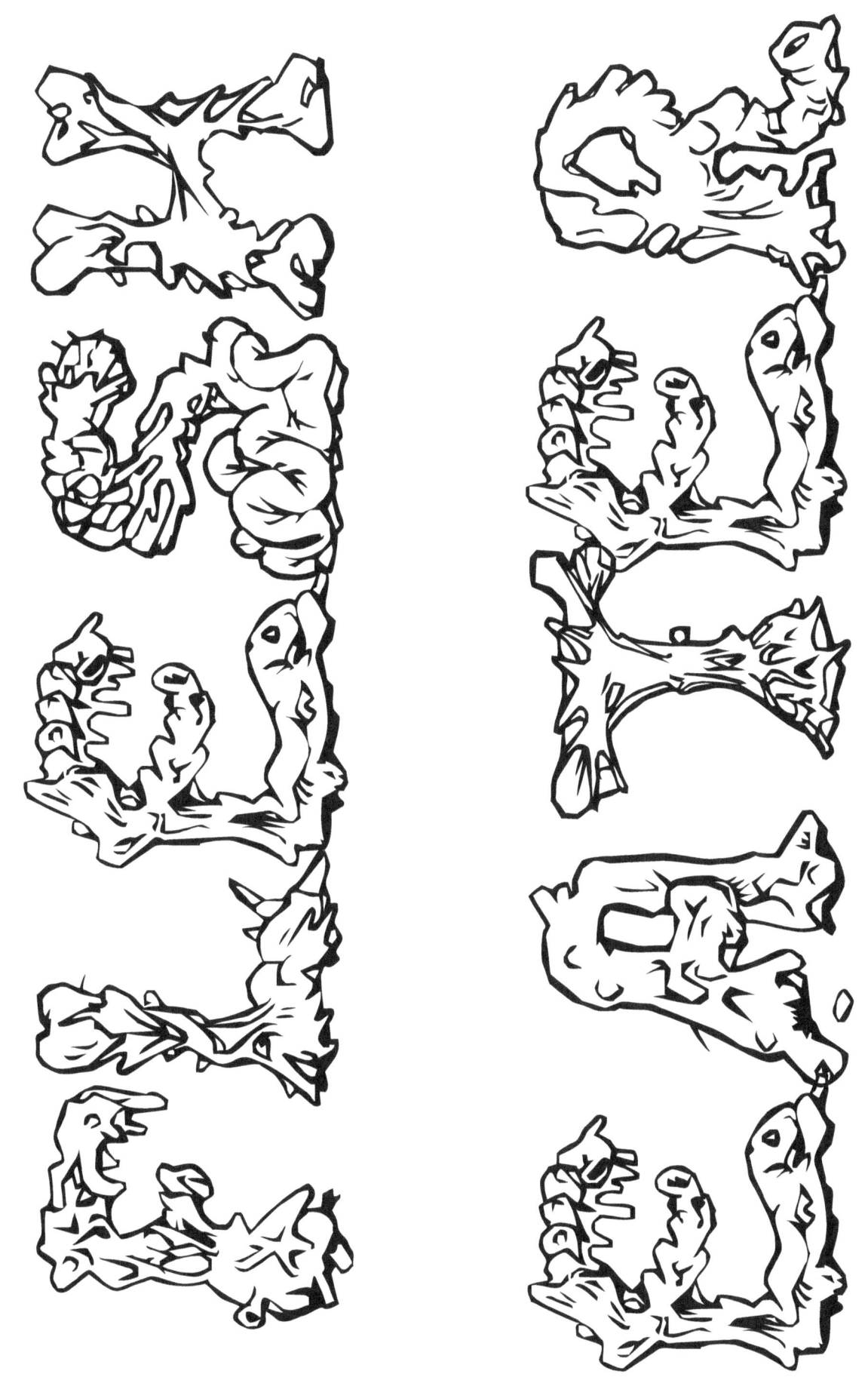

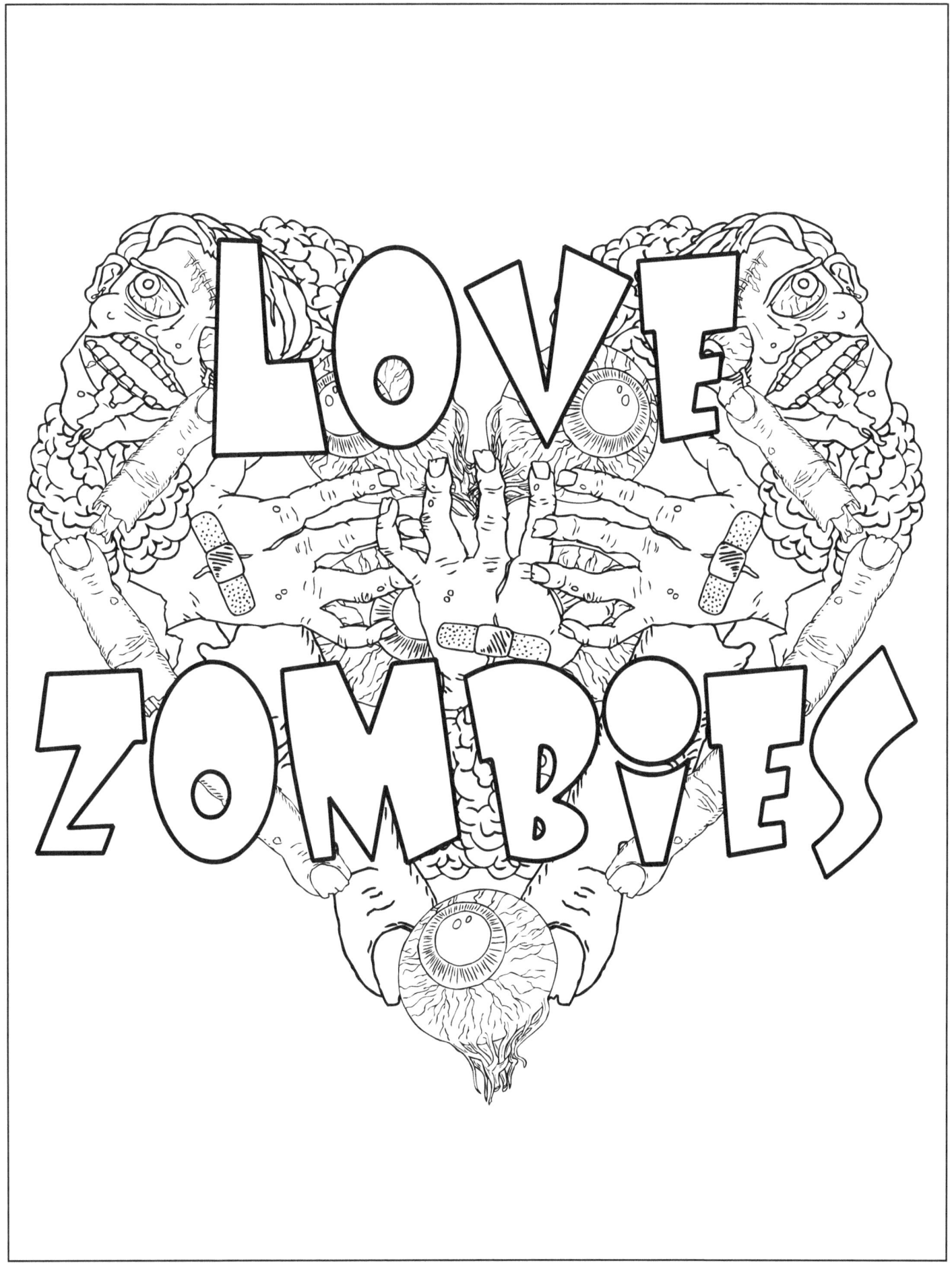

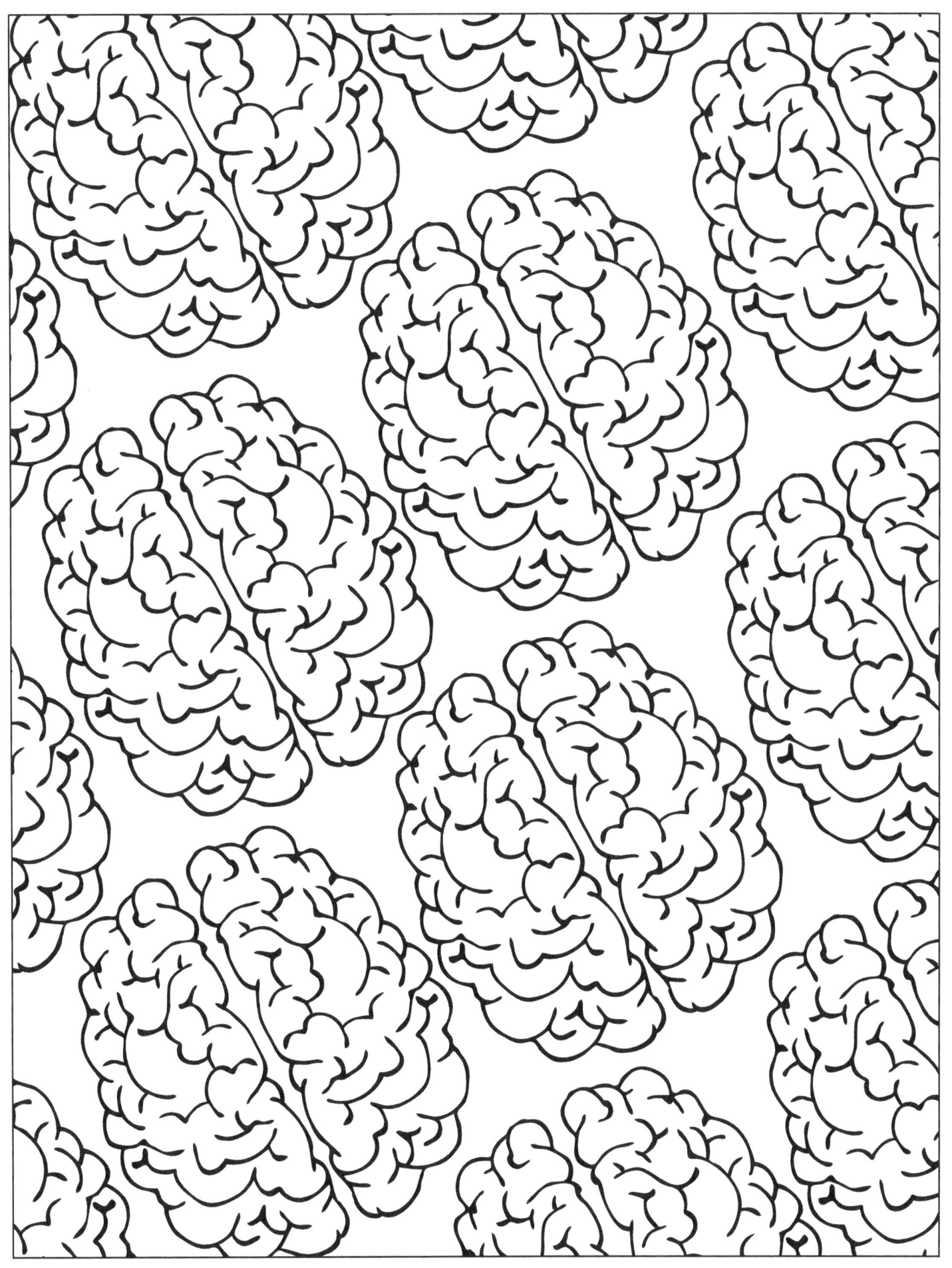

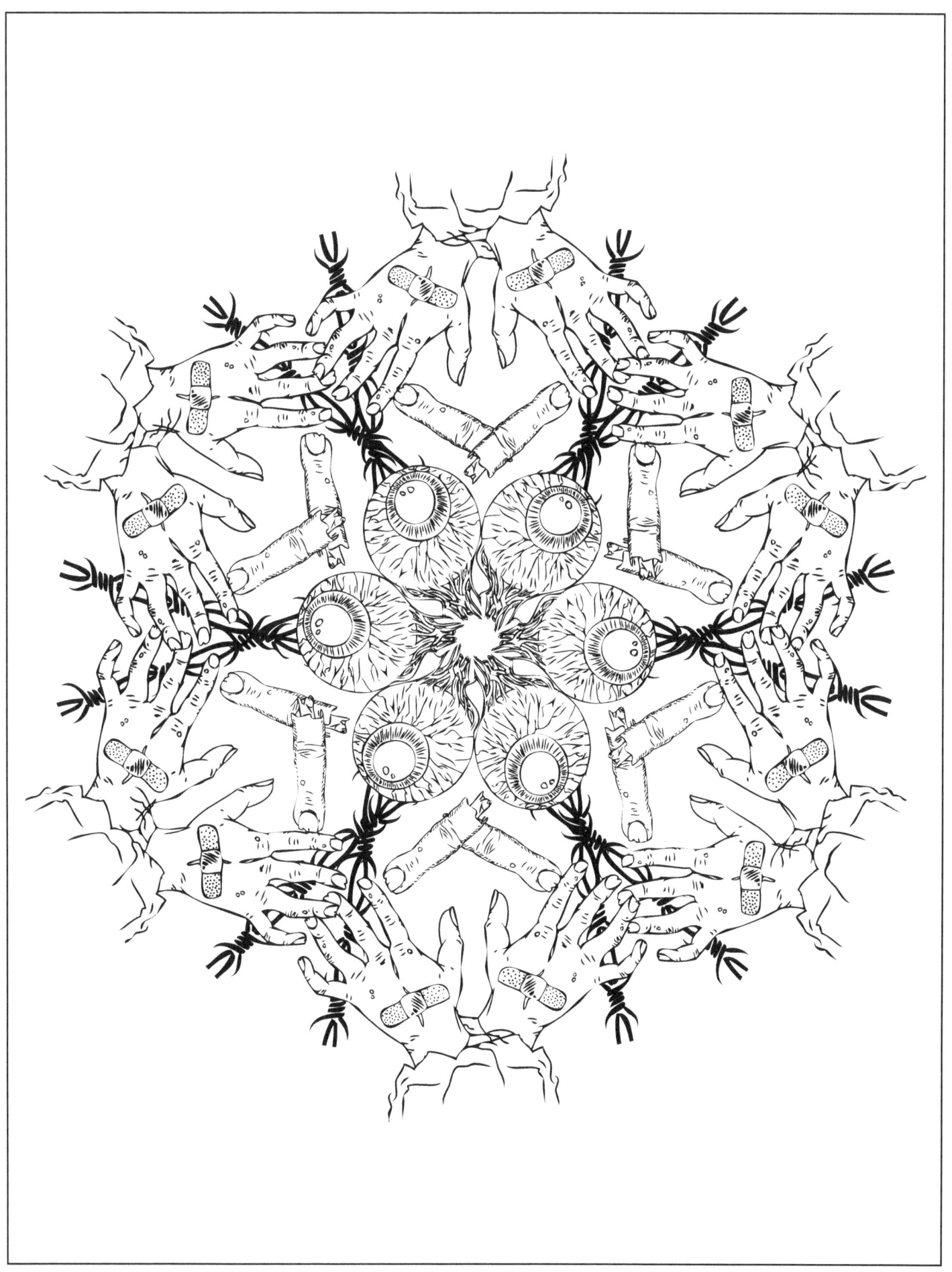

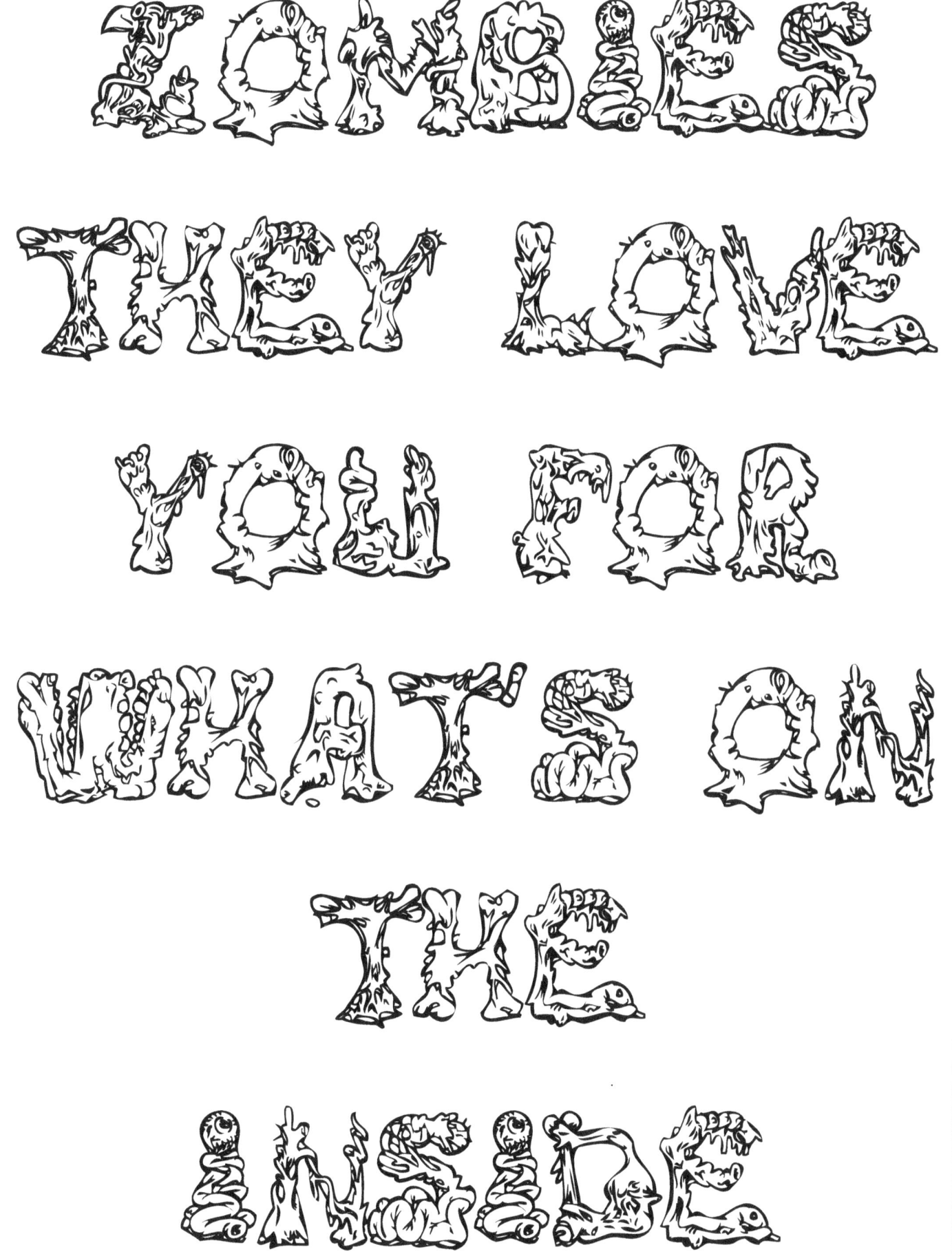

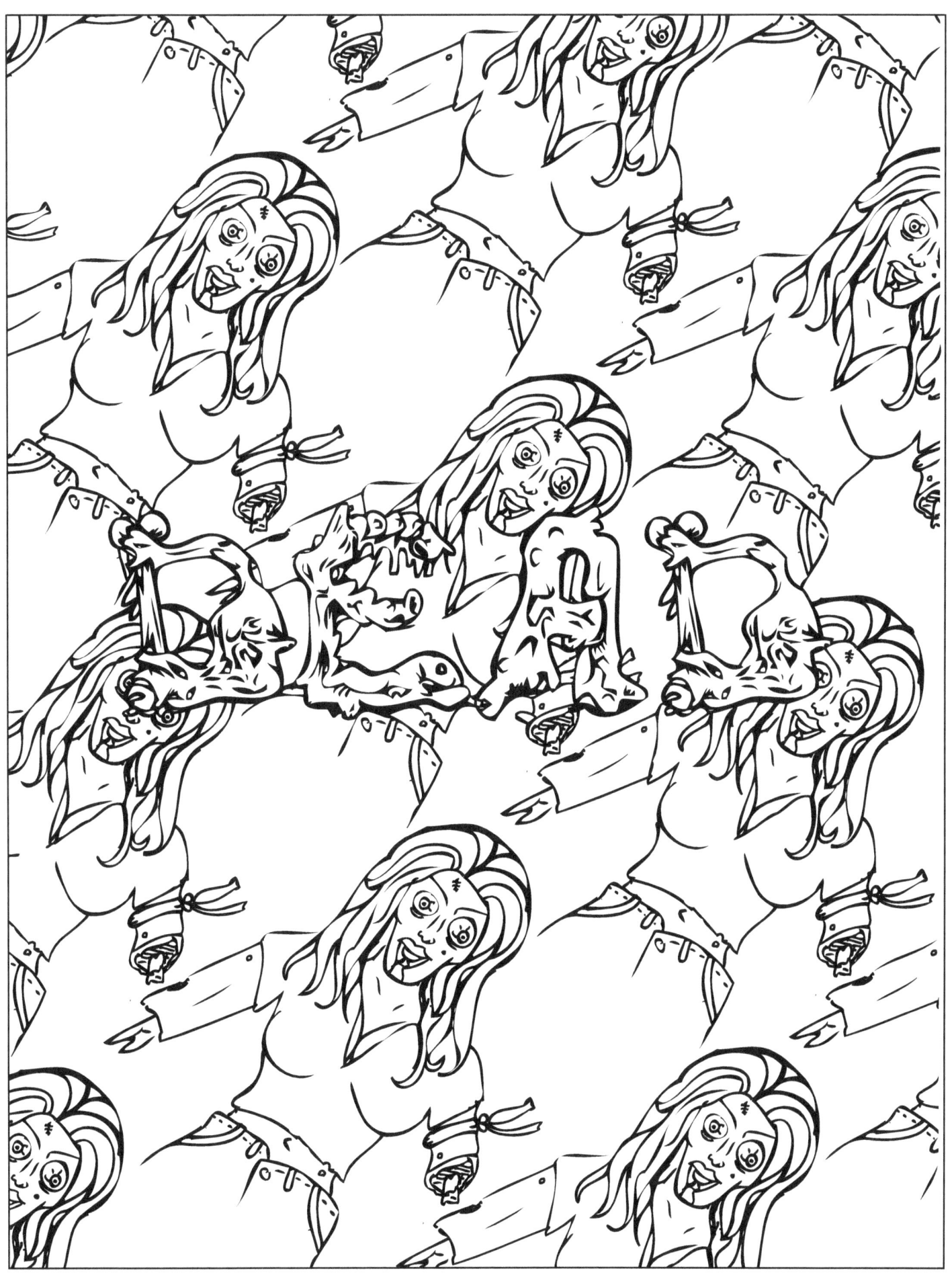

Zombies are the only men that will love you for your brains

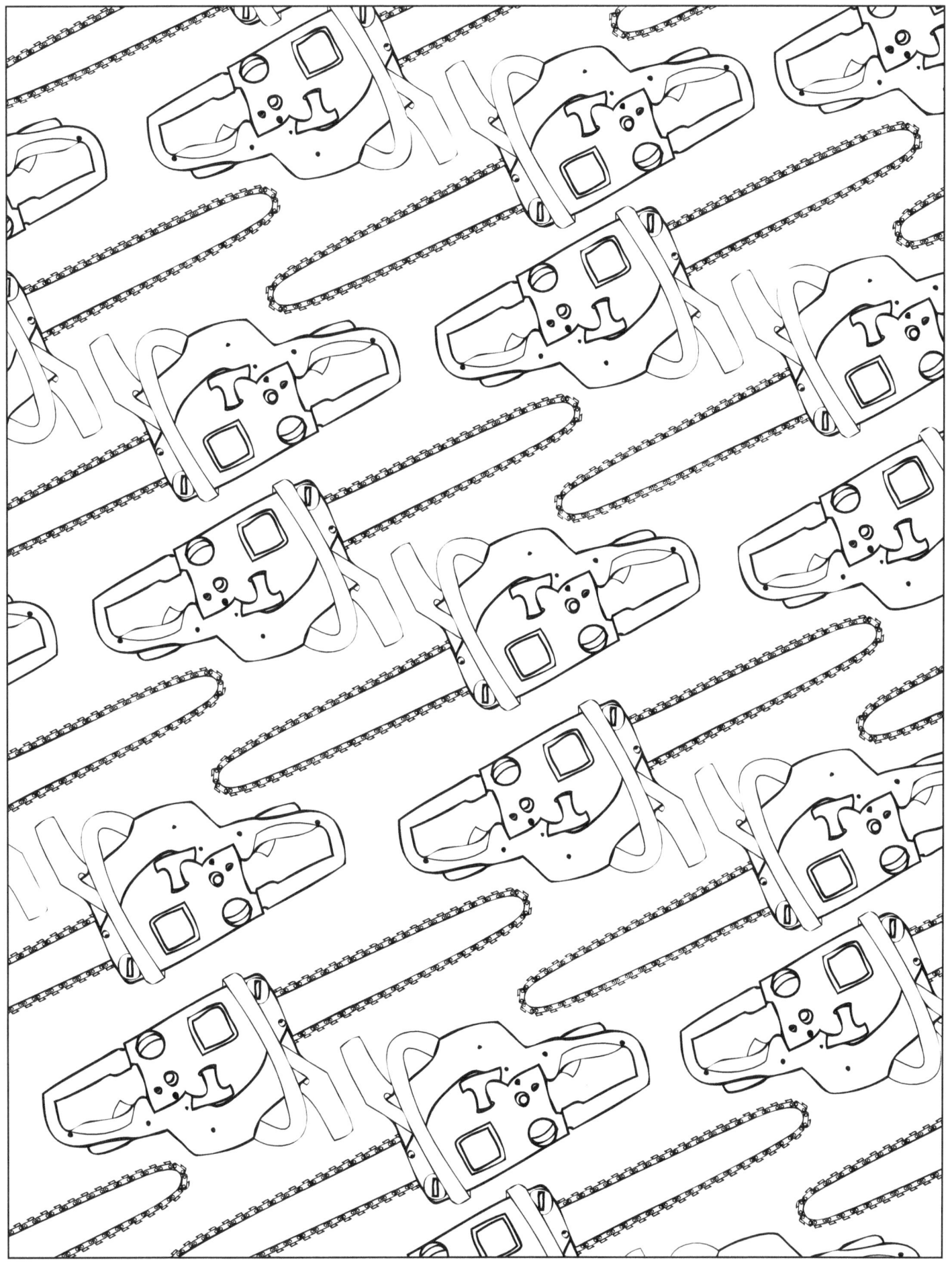

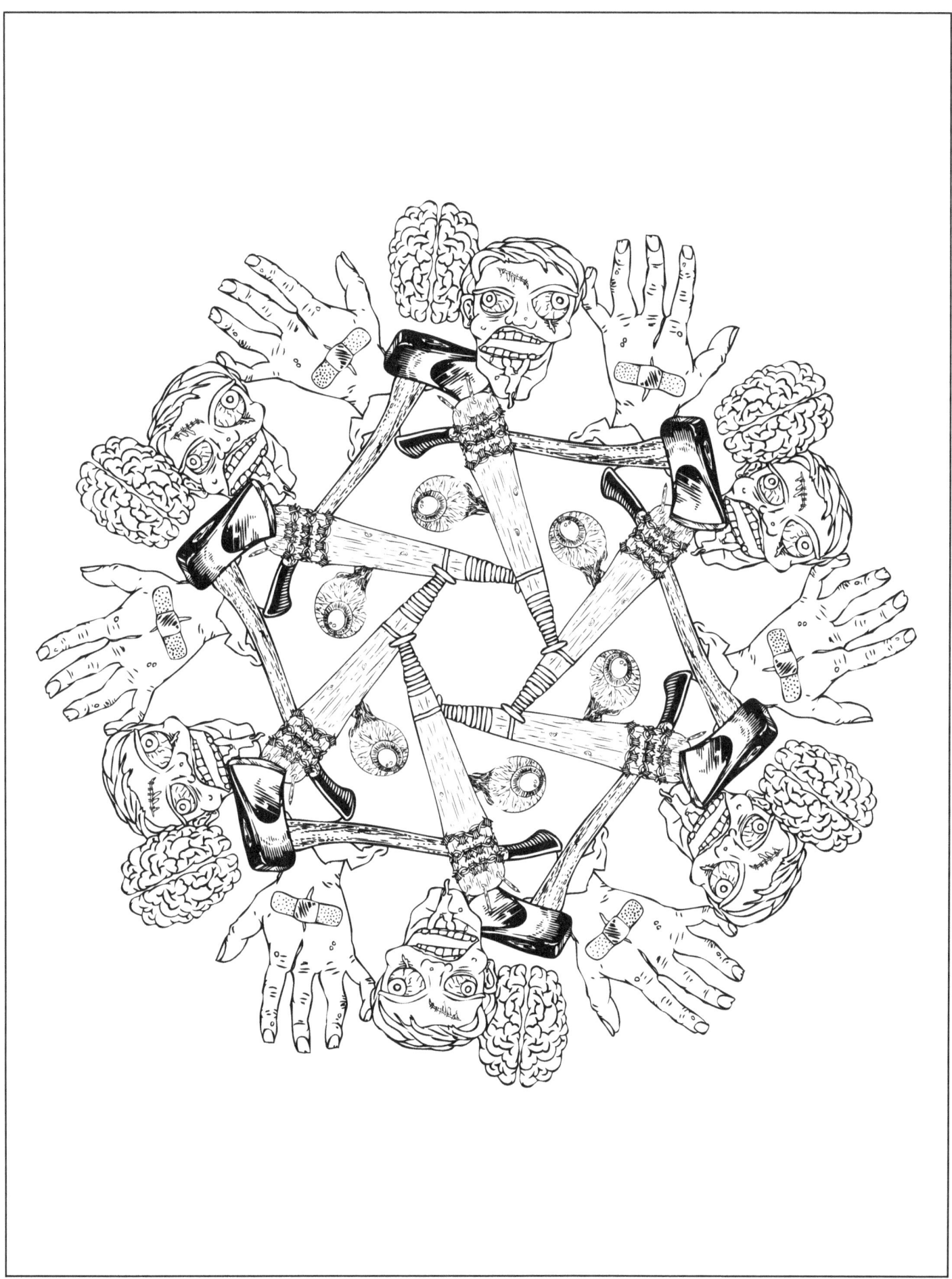

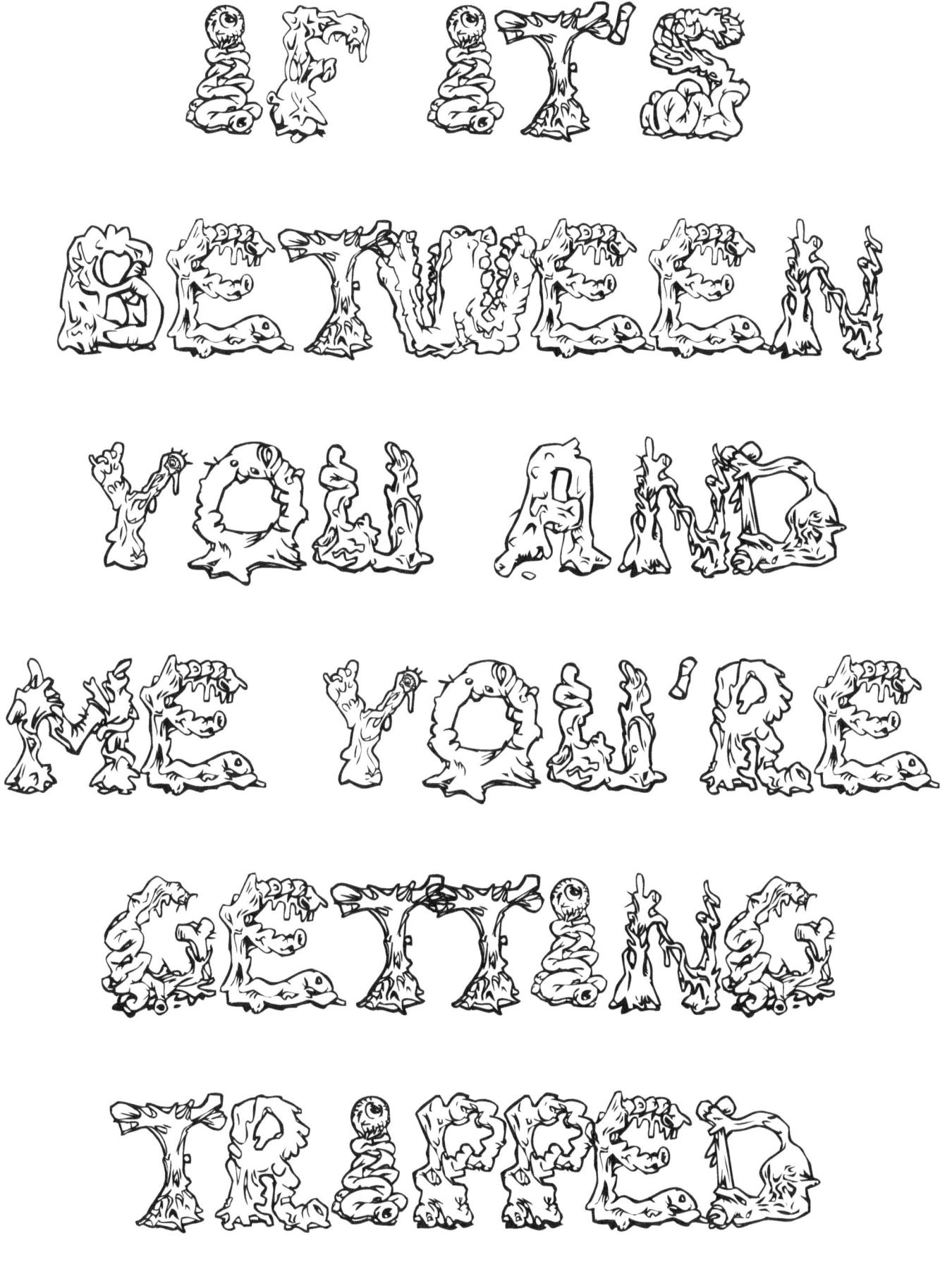

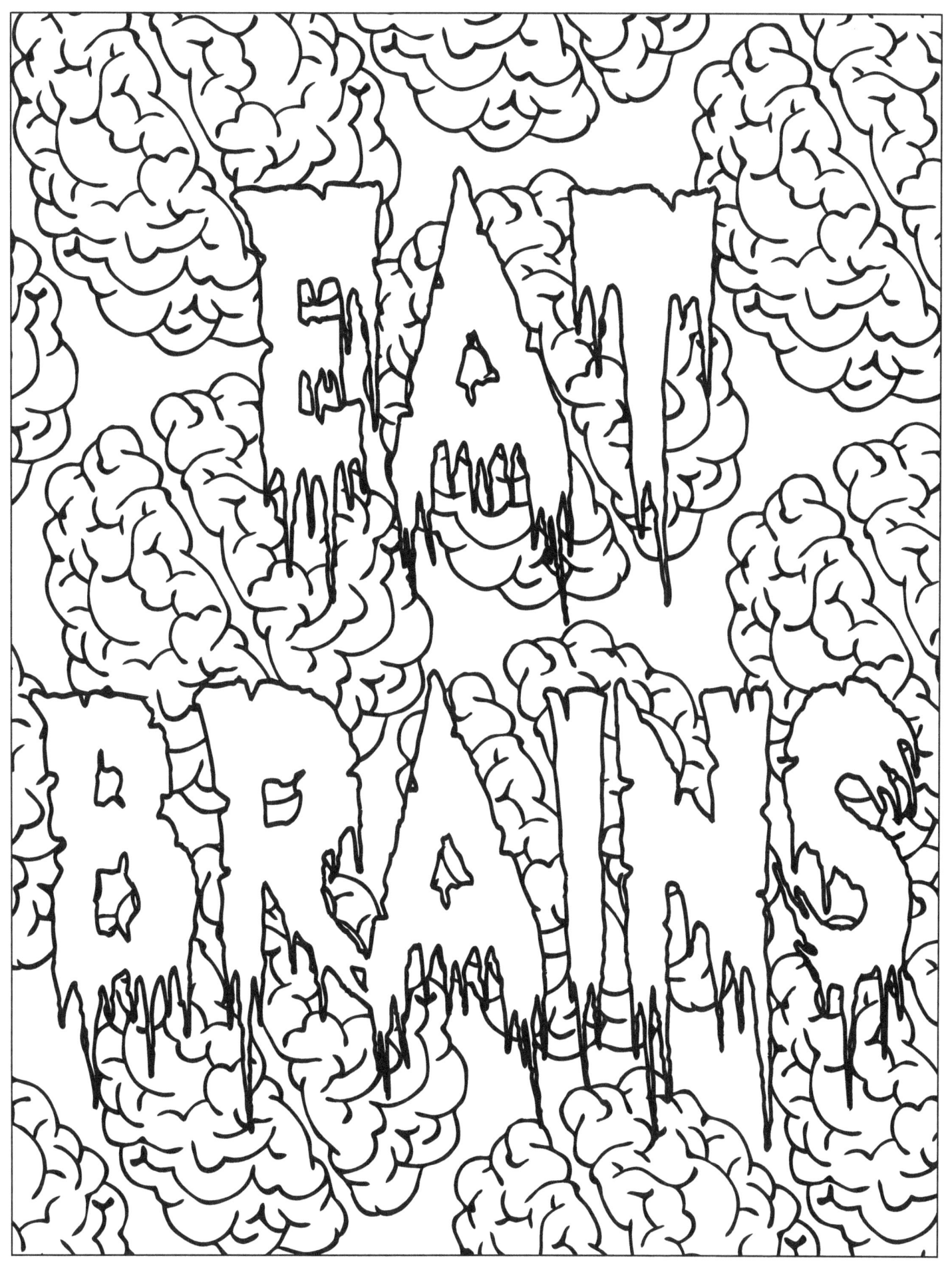

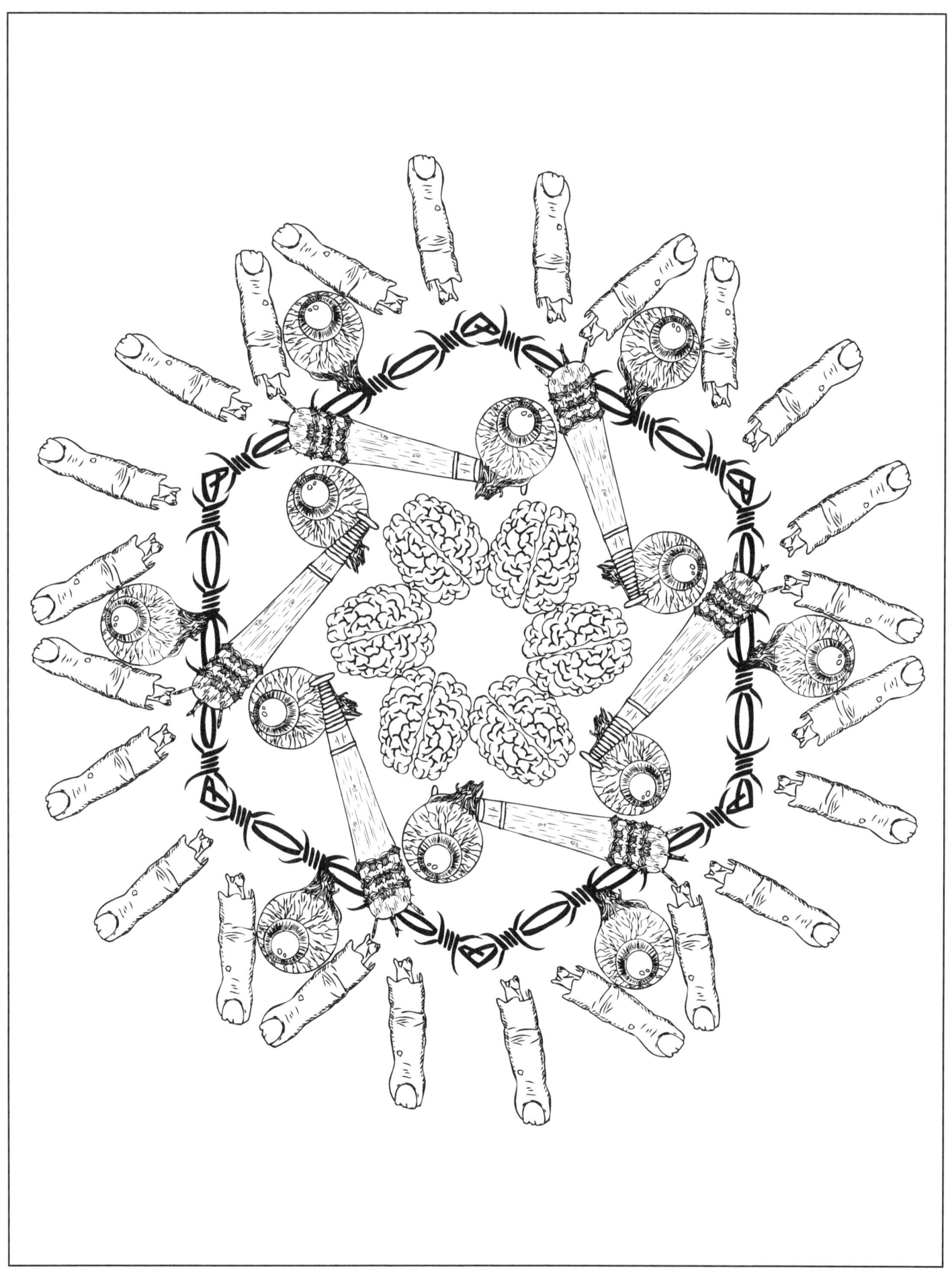

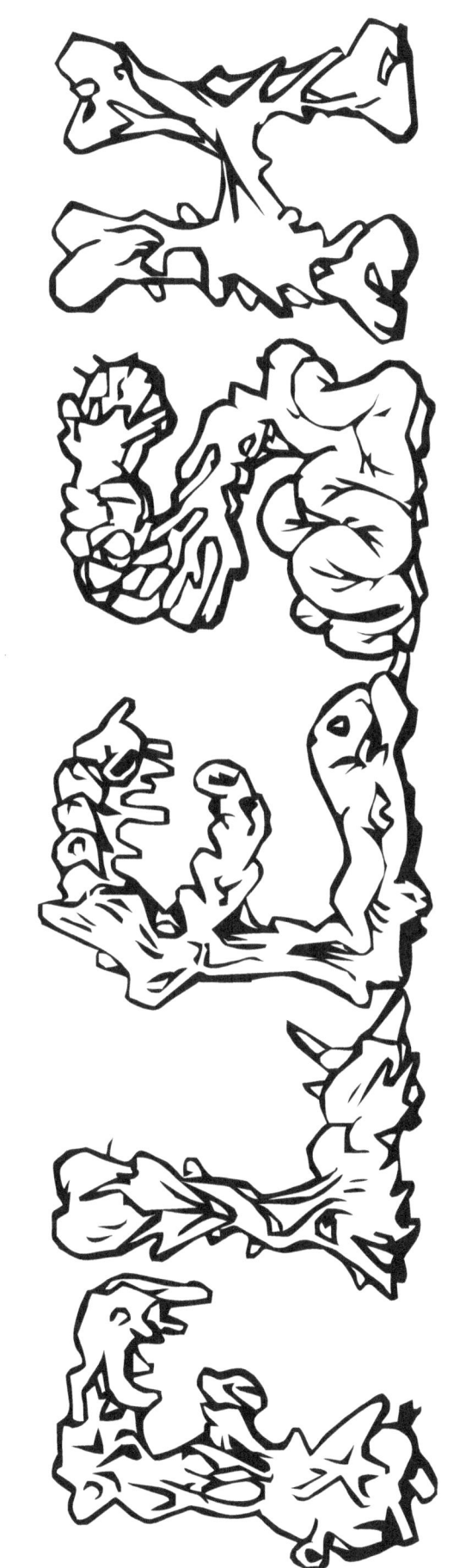
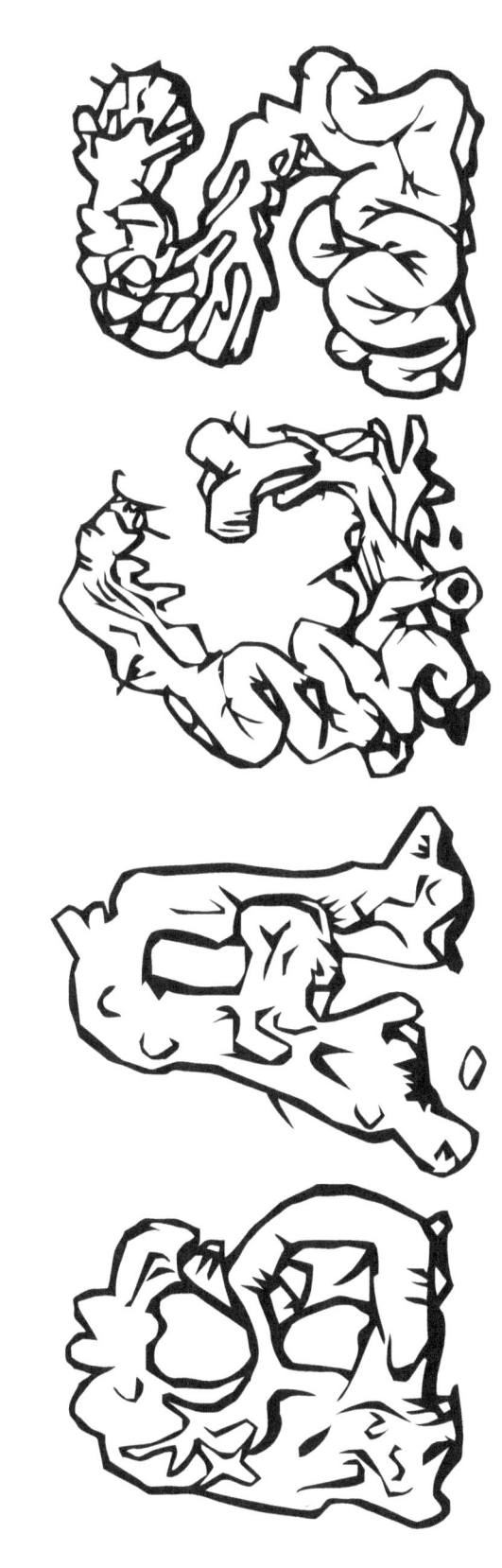

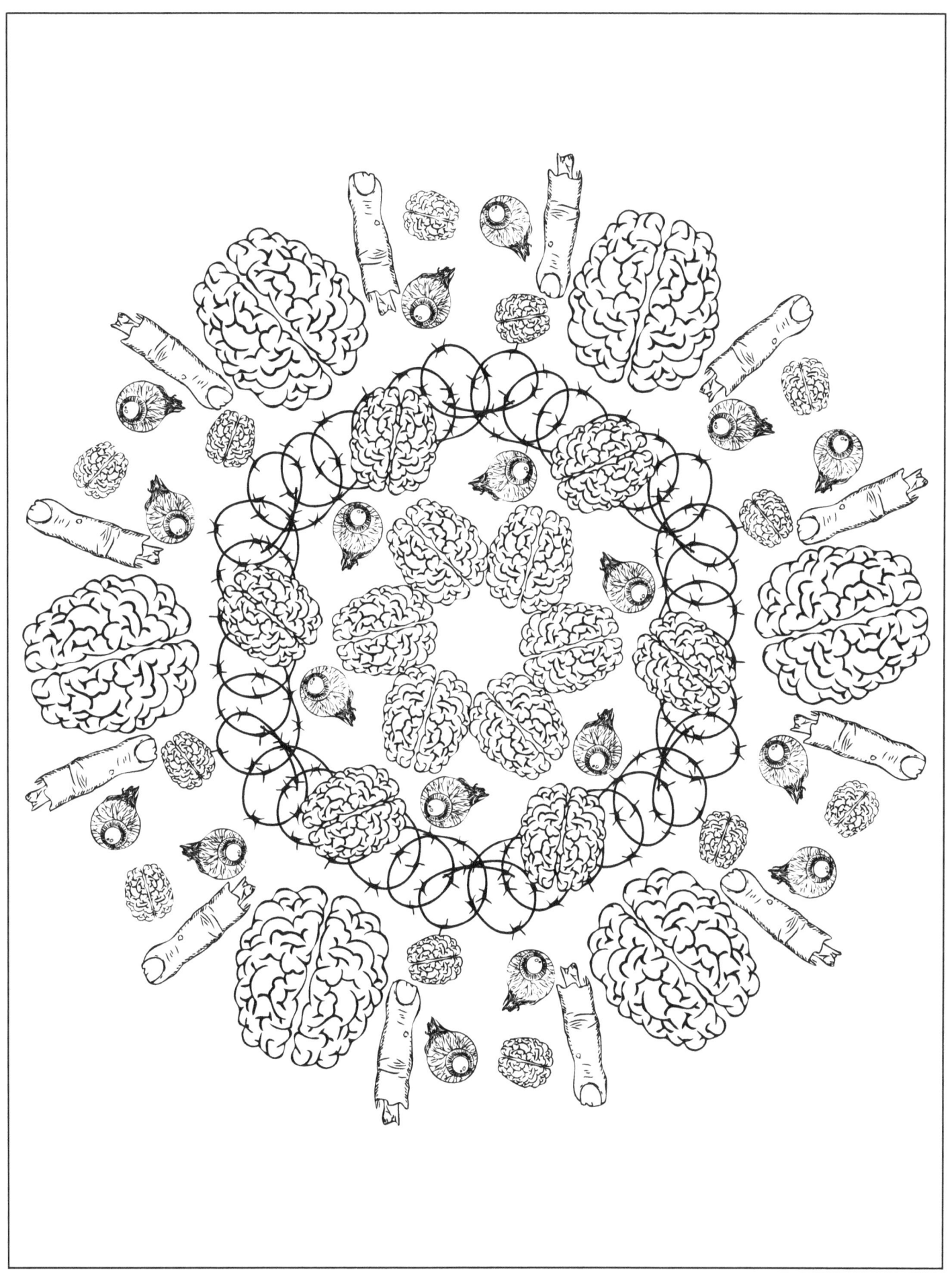

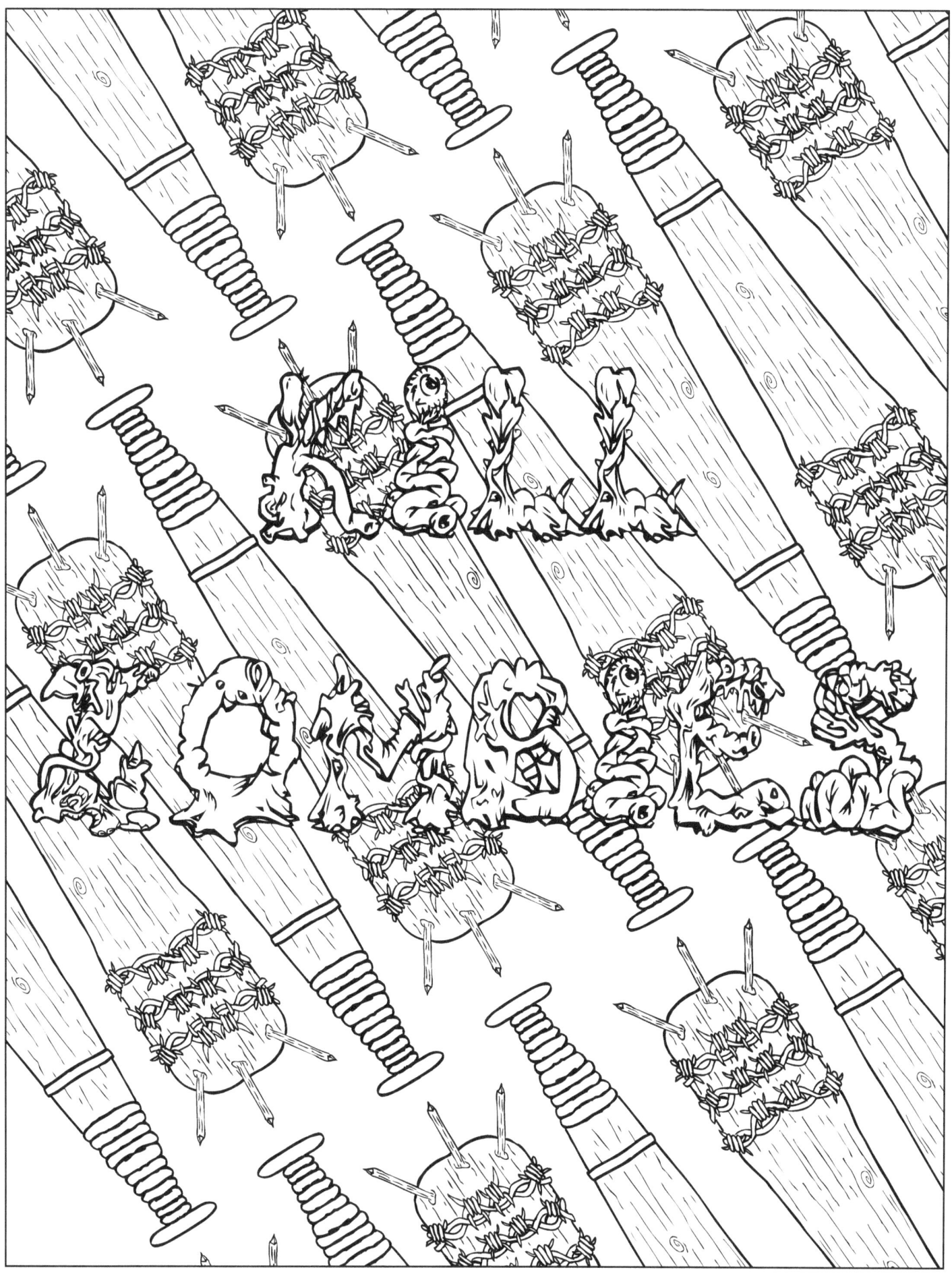

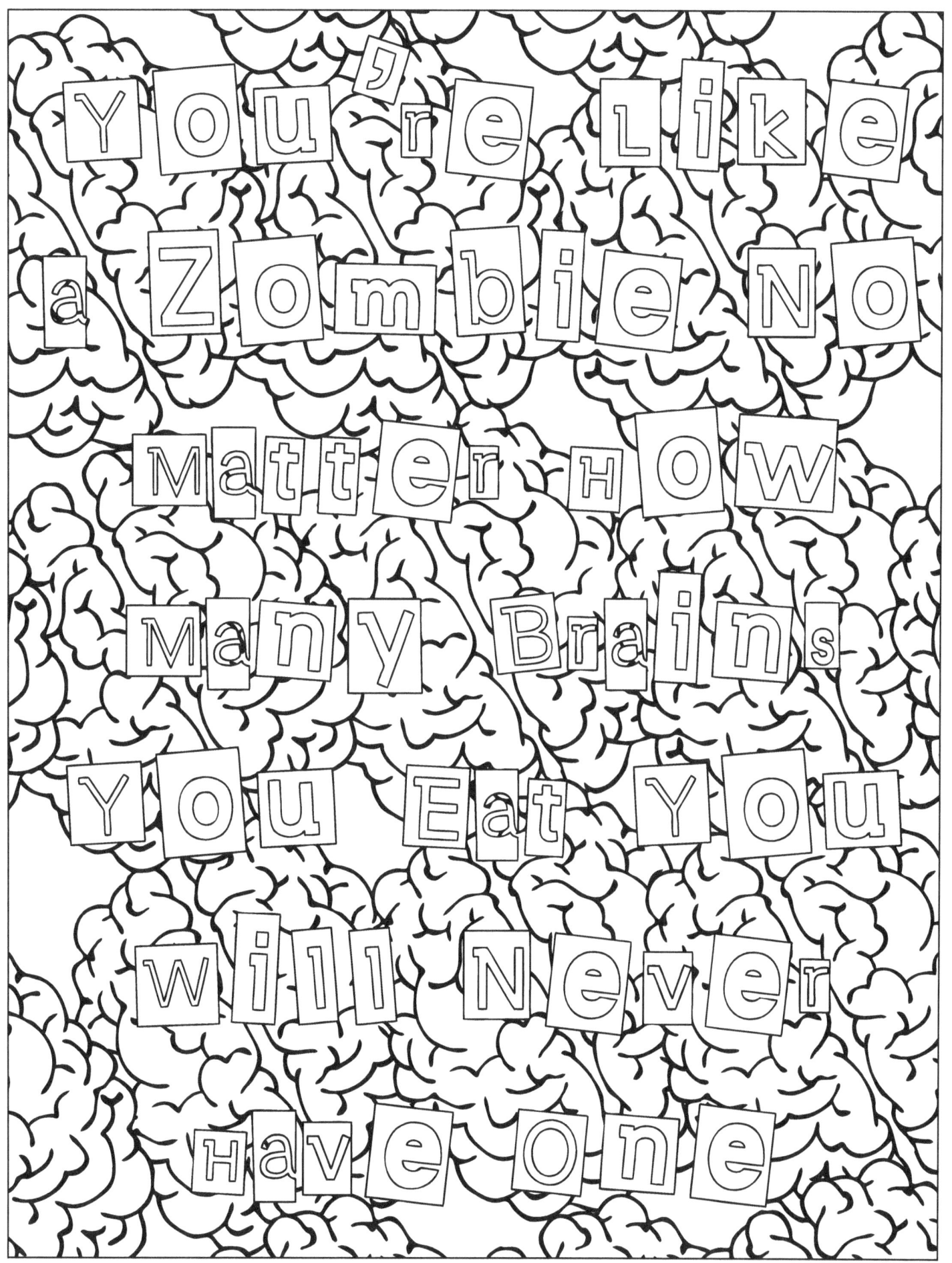

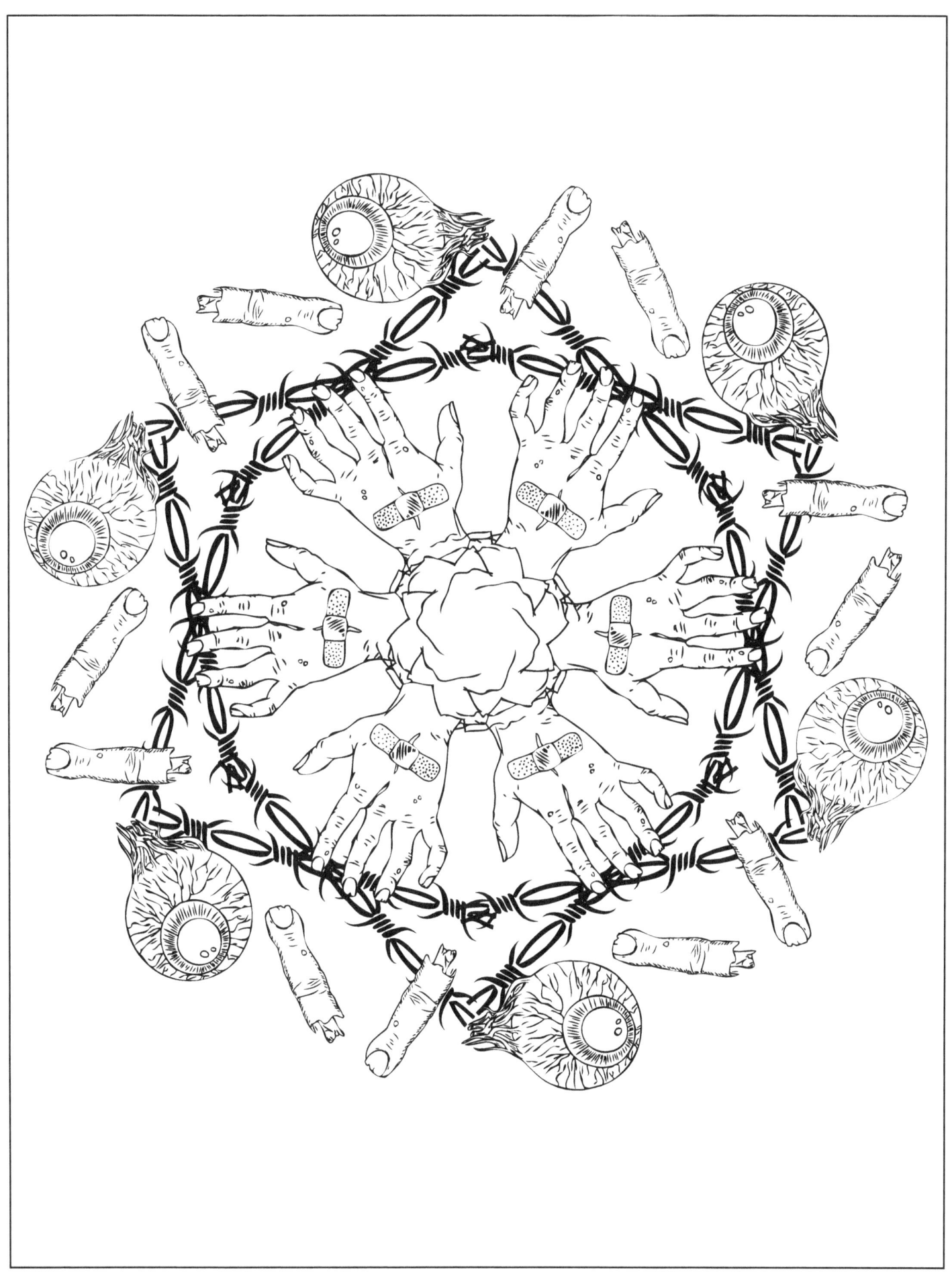

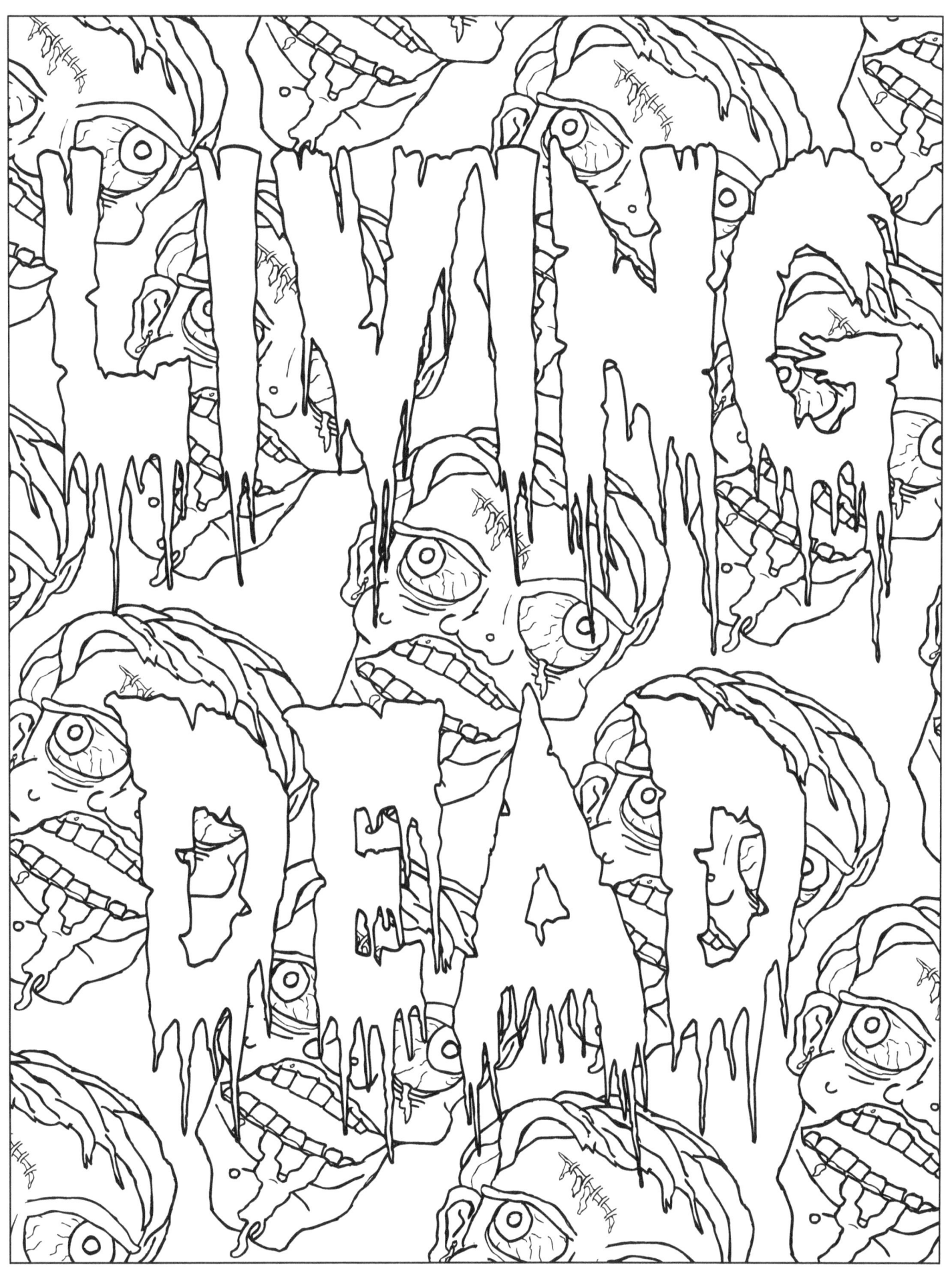

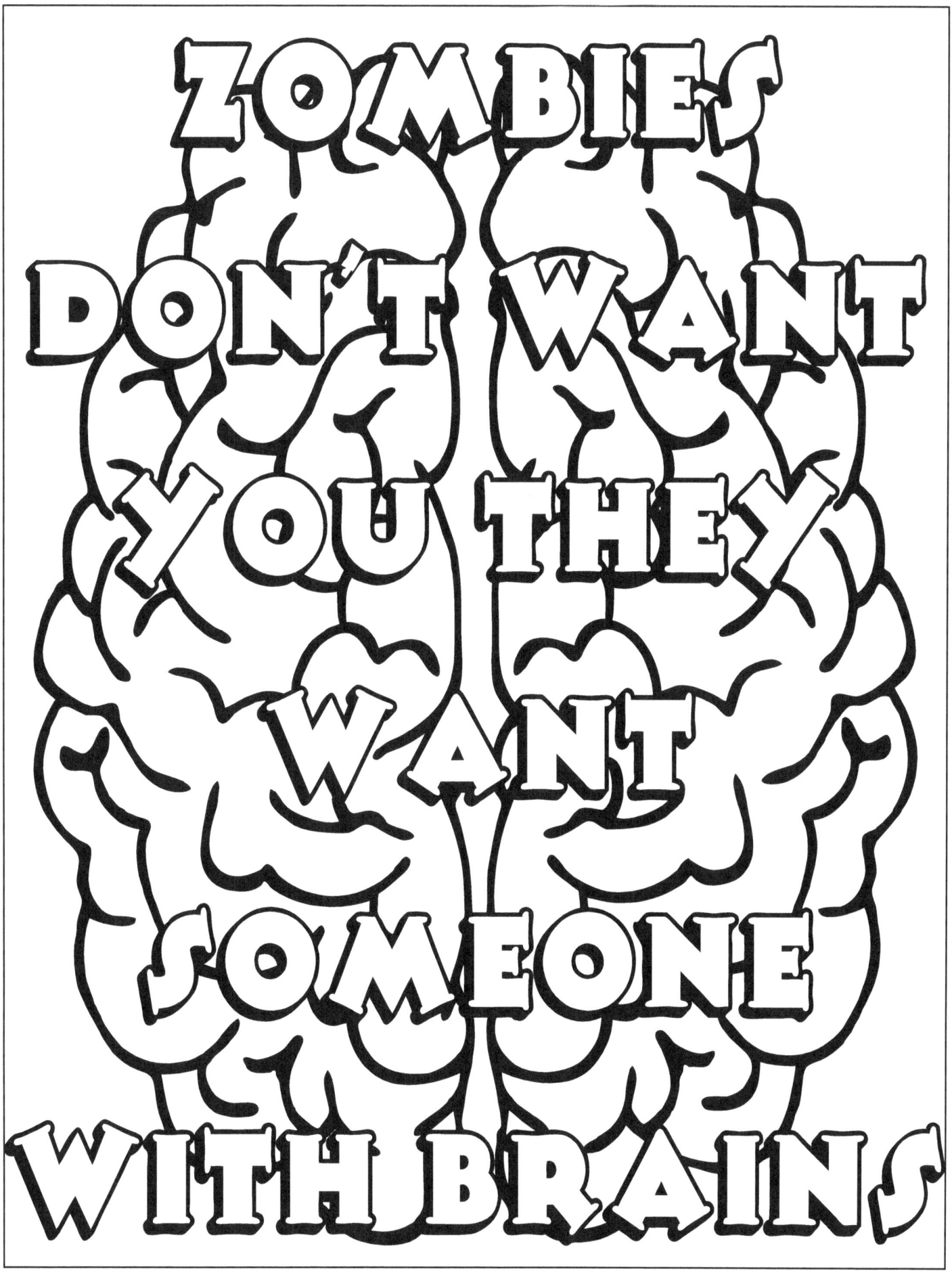

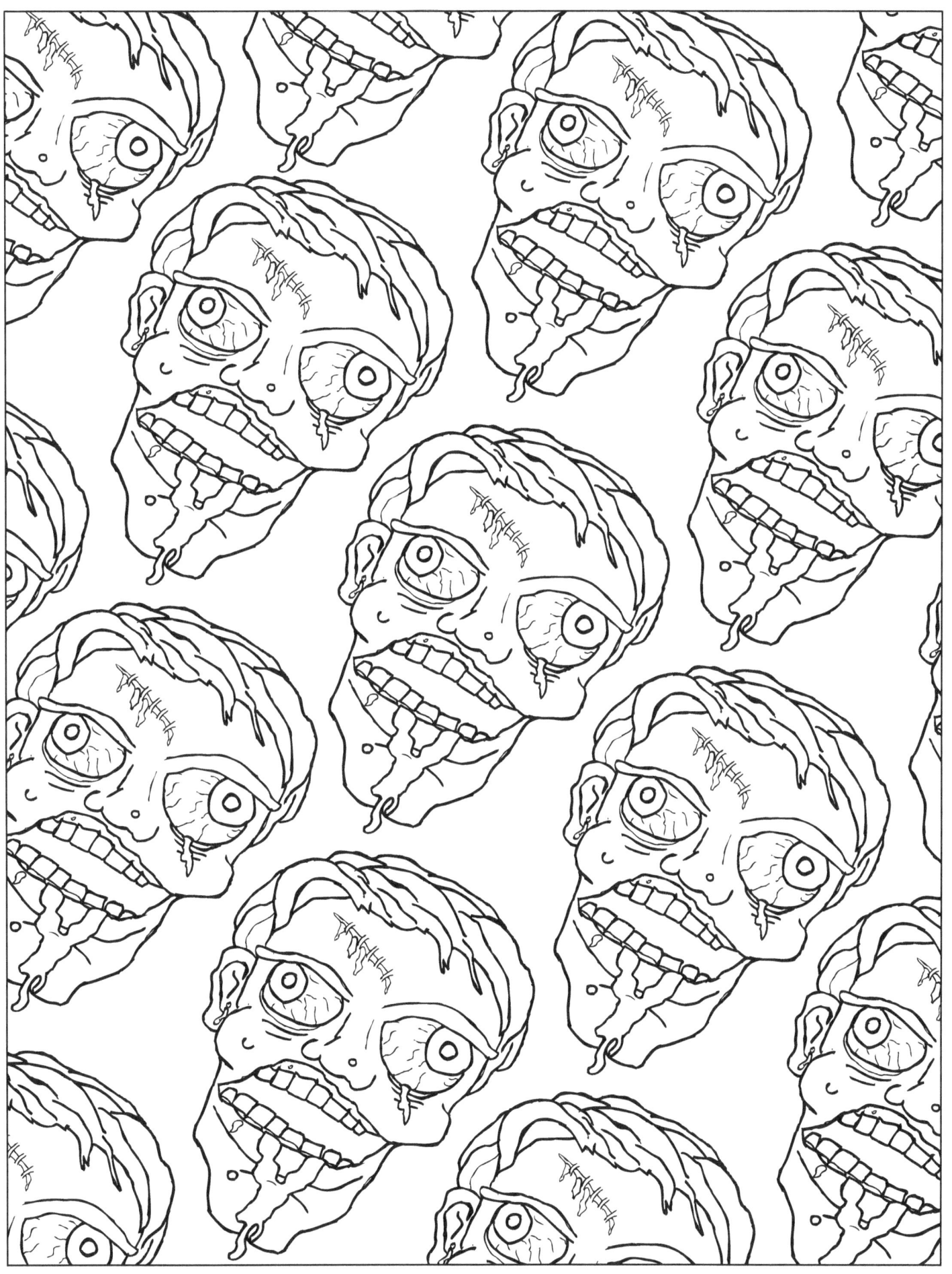

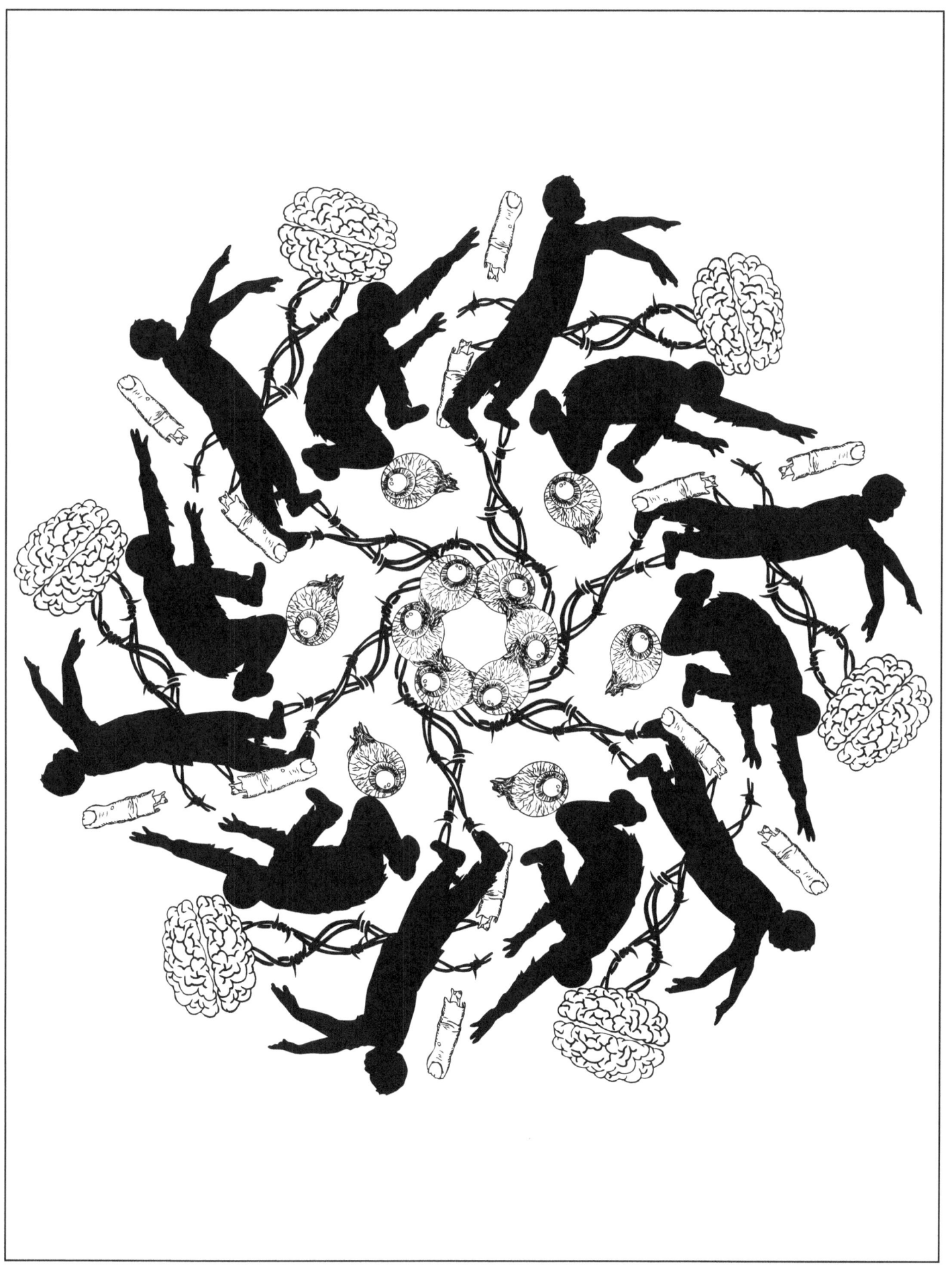

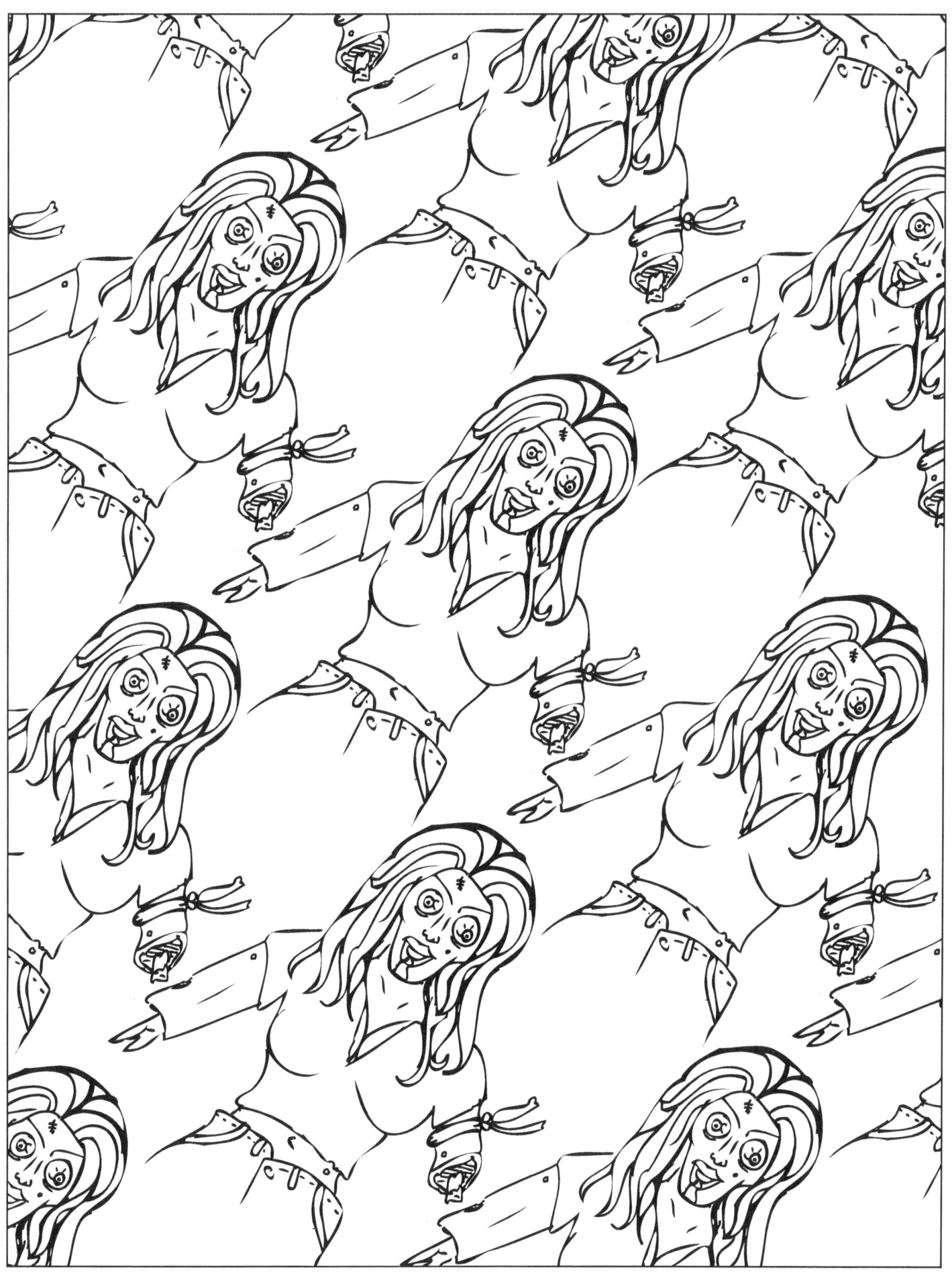